Clear Grammar 3
Student Workbook

Clear Grammar 3 Student Workbook

More Activities for Spoken and Written Communication

Keith S. Folse, Ph.D.
M.A. TESOL Program, University of Central Florida, Orlando

Kimberly Kalaydjian

April Muchmore-Vokoun
ESL Instructor, English Language Institute, University of South Florida

Elena Vestri Solomon
ESL, Hillsborough Community College

Ann Arbor

THE UNIVERSITY OF MICHIGAN PRESS

Contents

To the Teacher

Clear Grammar 3 Student Workbook is part of a multivolume series of grammar books for beginning to intermediate level students of English as a second or foreign language. Book 3 covers basic grammar points for intermediate nonnative speakers of English, including phrasal verbs, past progressive tense, present perfect tense, adverbs of manner, prepositions after verbs and adjectives, passive voice, relative clauses, infinitives and gerunds, connectors, and direct and indirect objects. This workbook may be used by students who are using the *Clear Grammar 3* textbook or any other similar grammar book. In addition, the workbook could be used by students in a conversation course so that they can have written practice to supplement the spoken practice in class.

The textbook for *Clear Grammar 3* contains grammar presentations using deductive and inductive approaches to accommodate the wide variety of learning styles that exist among language learners. In addition, the textbook contains an array of exercises and activities ranging from simple fill-in-the-blank exercises to original sentence creation and error identification and correction.

The exercises in the workbook have both writing and speaking practice for the grammar points. The exercises for each of the grammar points in the textbook are sequenced from controlled (easy) to more open (challenging) activities. However, the exercises and activities in this workbook provide a different kind of practice. The exercises in this book attempt to simulate real language situations through the use of realia, sentence study, puzzles, and more difficult objective (TOEFL-like) exercises. Thus, the exercises in this workbook offer a good complement to the exercises available in the student textbook.

The exercises in *Clear Grammar 3 Student Workbook* follow a similar format to facilitate use by both the teacher and the student. Each of the twelve units in this workbook offers these seven exercises:

Exercise 1. Realia
Exercise 2. Original Sentence Writing
Exercise 3. Realia
Exercise 4. Game, Puzzle, or Similar Activity
Exercise 5. Dialogue and Conversation Practice
Exercise 6. Sentence Study
Exercise 7. TOEFL Review

Exercises 1 and 3 are called **Realia.** In these exercises, students will work with postcards, newspaper articles, advertisements for various products, and other kinds of "real" examples of the grammar point being practiced in a particular unit.

Exercise 2, **Original Sentence Writing,** requires students to write their own unique sentences from prompts. The prompts either include specific examples of the grammar point being practiced, or they elicit use of the grammar point. For example, in unit 6 on prepositions after verbs and adjectives, students are provided with a list of questions that contain correct use of prepositions and are asked to write responses to the questions, whereas in unit 5 on adverbs of manner and related terms they are given sentences containing adjectives as prompts and asked to write sentences containing adverbs that correspond to the provided adjectives.

Exercise 4 is often some type of **game** or other **fun activity.** Learners practice the grammar point while doing some challenging activity. Exercise 4 often consists of a crossword puzzle, mini-mystery, or word search activity.

In Exercise 5, students work with original **dialogues** and **conversations.** If they are asked to write original dialogues, usually general guidelines or parameters are given, such as the names of the two people in the dialogue as well as their relationship (e.g., good friends who haven't seen each other in a long time, driving instructor and students, two sisters). In addition, students are sometimes told exactly what problem to develop (and solve!) in the dialogue. For example, the directions for exercise 5 in unit 11 on VERB + direct or indirect object instruct the students to write a dialogue in which a brother and a sister are having a disagreement about what to buy their mother for her birthday. When students are asked to read a dialogue, instead of writing their own, the dialogue helps learners by providing a clear example of how native speakers of English might use the grammar points in real conversation. This exercise provides practice not only in using the structures but also in listening for them in conversation. Thus, this exercise gives students practice in speaking and listening (as well as in writing and reading).

Exercise 6 is called **Sentence Study.** In this exercise, students must first read a given sentence or minidialogue that contains elements of the grammar points being studied in that particular unit. Next, students are to read four sentences and choose which one or ones are true based on the information in the original sentences. This exercise is a very important one because it not only helps learners sort out what the grammar point really means but also promotes critical thinking skills in English. In addition, it promotes reading skills in English through more rapid recognition of the given grammar structures.

Exercise 7 provides a **review** of the language points in the unit using objective questions of two types. Resembling questions found in the structure section of the Test of English as a Foreign Language (TOEFL), the questions in this exercise employ a multiple-choice format. There are two parts. In Part 1, there are eight questions that students are to complete with the correct answer by choosing among four answers provided. In Part 2, there are seven questions that contain four underlined words or phrases. In this part of the exercise, students are to choose the one underlined word or phrase that has a grammatical error in it. While students are not required to actually correct the error, teachers may find it more beneficial to ask students to do so.

Unit 1

Review of Book 2

Exercise 1. **Realia** Below is a short article that might appear in a history magazine. However, it must be correct before it is published. There are ten mistakes. Circle the mistakes, and write a correction in the space above each one.

Helen Keller was the American author and lecturer who was born in 1880. Helen was born a normal, healthy child. However, when she was nineteen months old, she becomed very ill. This illness caused her to become deaf and blind. In Helens time, this meant that she would be unable to communicate with anyone for the rest of her life. As a result, Helen's parents were not able to teach she anything for the first seven years of her life. Helen eventually became wilder many of the animals that surrounded her country home.

When Helen had seven years old, something happened that would change her entire life. Anne Sullivan, a teacher who had been blind and now could not see very well, came to live with Helen and her family. Anne's too difficult job was to try to teach Helen how to behave like a normal child. After much hard work, Anne teached Helen how to use sign language. This allowed Helen to experience a whole new world. She was finally able to speak to her parents and communicate with the people around her.

Helen managed to accomplish many things in her lifetime. When she was twenty years old, she did entered Radcliffe College. With Annes' help as a translator, Helen was able to take classes with hearing and sighted people. In 1904, Helen graduated as one of the top students in her class. In her lifetime, Helen wrote 13 books, one of which was translated into more than 50 different languages. She was also a world traveler who visited a variety of countries. These achievements have been an inspiration to people around the world.

Exercise 2. **Original Sentence Writing** Answer each of the following questions using a complete sentence.

1. When are you going to graduate from high school?

   (OR: When did you graduate from high school?)

   _____

2. How often do you go to the movies?

   _____

3. When did you last go out for dinner at a restaurant?

   _____

4. Did your teacher give your class a test last week? (use an object pronoun)

   _____

5. What advice would you give someone who is going to go out into the rain?

   _____

6. What is one thing that you do better than anyone else?

   _____

7. How often are you late for class?

   _____

8. Which tastes better to you—chocolate or vanilla ice cream?

   _____

Exercise 3. **Realia** Angela goes to the grocery store once a week to buy food. Look at the two grocery receipts below. Use them to answer the questions that follow. Answer in complete sentences.

```
Happy Time Grocery                Happy Time Grocery
March 7                           March 14

milk (one gallon)  3.75          coffee            3.99
bread               .99          tomato            1.25
chicken            6.99          hamburger         4.58
lettuce            1.99          broccoli          2.38
cereal             4.99          bagels            1.50
cookies            2.34          soup               .99
fish               7.38          dog food         10.00
frozen pizza       4.50
ice cream          3.59          Subtotal         24.69
tomato             1.19          Plus tax          1.72
green pepper        .89          Total            26.41

Subtotal          38.60
Plus tax           2.70
Total             41.30
```

1. How much did Angela spend on groceries on March 7?

   _____

2. What was the most expensive thing that Angela bought on March 7?

   _____

3. What food cost the same as the bread?

   _____

4. On March 14, what food was more expensive than the fish was on March 7?

   _____

5. Which day was cheaper for Angela?

   _____

6. How much money did Angela spend for both trips to the store?

   _____

7. How much did a gallon of milk cost?

   _____

8. What did Angela buy both times?

   _____

Exercise 4.   **Puzzle/Game** Read the clues for the crossword puzzle. Then fill in the answers in the puzzle. Two items have been done for you.

Across

3. We _____ Dina at the mall yesterday. She looked really happy.

4. The soup is _____ hot. It needs to cool a little before we can eat it.

7. They _____ remember to bring their homework. They always leave it at home.

8. Alex _____ that we were meeting at 6:00 P.M. That is why he was late.

9. How _____ time do we have before class starts?

10. Gianni and Marcus _____ soccer last night for two hours.

11. Are you going to see Jim today? Can you give _____ this book for me?

Down

1. That was the _____ test the grammar teacher has ever given! Everyone got 100!

2. I _____ my purse in the restaurant. We have to go back and get it.

5. Diana _____ her friend to the party last night. He was very funny.

6. It might rain today. I think you _____ take an umbrella with you.

12. My brother likes only the _____ expensive cars. He wants to own a Ferrari or a Rolls Royce.

13. Jeannie is making cookies _____ her daughter. Rachel loves to eat them.

Across

15. In Florida, it is _____ too hot to go

    outside. When that happens, people will

    stay inside and run their air conditioners.

Down

14. Elena is making too much noise. Please

    tell _____ to be more quiet.

Exercise 5.   `Dialogue and Conversation Practice` Martin and Andrew are talking
about trips they would like to take. Complete each sentence by
circling the word or phrase that best completes each sentence.

Martin: If you could travel anywhere you wanted, where would it be?

Andrew: Well, I have always wanted to visit ❶ (a, an, the, ∅) Egypt.

Martin: Really? Why ❷ (did you want, do you want, are you wanting) to go
there?

Andrew: I've always wanted to take a cruise on ❸ (a, an, the) Nile River and
visit ❹ (a, an, the, ∅) famous Sphinx.

Martin: I guess that would be exciting. Unfortunately, I don't like places that are ❺
(very, much) hot. Egypt is definitely one of the ❻ (hot, hotter, hottest) places I
know. Can you think of a ❼ (cool, cooler, coolest) place to visit?

Andrew: Hmmmmm. You ❽ (should, must, will) go to Antarctica. That's the
❾ (cold, colder, coldest) place I can think of.

Martin: Yeah! That is a ❿ (very, too) cold place! If I go there, I am sure that I
⓫ (should, might, will) see many different kinds of animals. I have
⓬ (always, rarely, never) wanted to see a polar bear. I could see one there!

Andrew: No, you will ⓭ (always, sometimes, never) see a polar bear at the South Pole.
You can only see ⓮ (the, one, another) at the North Pole.

Martin: Oh. I ⓯ (don't know, didn't know, am not knowing) that. Can I see
⓰ (a, an, the, ∅) penguins there?

Andrew: Yup.

Martin: OK. Well, I guess I will still go then!

Extra Writing Practice

On another sheet of paper, write a dialogue between two people
in which the topic is an interesting place that you (one of you or
both of you) have visited. Be sure to skip a line between each
person's sentences. Try to practice the grammar that you studied
in Unit 1.

Exercise 6. **Sentence Study** Read the beginning sentences. Then read the answer choices and put a check mark in front of **all of the sentences that are true** based on the beginning sentences. Remember that more than one answer is possible sometimes.

1. Mary thinks that it is too hot in the house, but John is comfortable.
   ___ a. The temperature is just right for John.
   ___ b. The room is not cool enough for Mary.
   ___ c. Mary thinks the house is hotter than it should be.
   ___ d. Mary and John both think the temperature is fine.

2. That is a pretty glass vase, but this antique silver bowl is even more beautiful.
   ___ a. The vase is more beautiful than the bowl.
   ___ b. The vase is made of glass.
   ___ c. The bowl is an antique.
   ___ d. The bowl isn't as pretty as the vase.

3. We thought Sue's party was on Saturday night, but it was really on Friday night.
   ___ a. The party on Friday was better than the one on Saturday.
   ___ b. We were mistaken about the date for the party.
   ___ c. The party took place on Friday night.
   ___ d. The party that we organized was on Friday night.

4. Marty's uncle is a lot more fun to talk to than Sarah's is.
   ___ a. Marty has an uncle.
   ___ b. It is more fun to talk to Sarah's aunt.
   ___ c. Sarah likes to talk to Marty's uncle.
   ___ d. Both relatives are very interesting to talk to.

5. We needed two cups of sugar for this recipe, but we only had one. It isn't as sweet as it should be.
   ___ a. The dessert is very sweet.
   ___ b. The dessert could be sweeter than it is.
   ___ c. Sugar isn't necessary for this recipe.
   ___ d. We added only half of the necessary sugar.

6. I spilled ketchup on my white shirt, so I have to put on my other one.
   ___ a. I have two white shirts.
   ___ b. One white shirt is dirty.
   ___ c. I need to change my shirt.
   ___ d. I was making ketchup.

7. Gina's little brother hates the taste of oysters, so he refuses to eat them.
   ___ a. Gina's brother never eats oysters.
   ___ b. Gina doesn't like the taste of oysters.
   ___ c. He doesn't like to eat with them.
   ___ d. He refuses to eat with his sister.

8. Roberto thinks that Rome is a much more interesting city than London.
   ___ a. Roberto likes London less than he likes Rome.
   ___ b. In Roberto's opinion, Rome isn't as interesting as London.
   ___ c. Of the two cities, Roberto would probably rather visit London.
   ___ d. According to Roberto, Rome is more interesting than London.

Exercise 7.   **TOEFL Review**

Part 1.   Completion. For items 1 through 8, circle the letter of the answer that best completes the statement.

1. Marcos baked ___ pies for Thanksgiving dinner.

   a. a pumpkin

   b. pumpkins

   c. an pumpkin

   d. some pumpkin

2. We ___ go to the movies tonight. Do you want to come?

   a. are going

   b. am going

   c. are going to

   d. am going to

3. ___ will you be gone on vacation? I'll be gone two weeks.

   a. How much

   b. How long

   c. How far

   d. How many

4. Jonathan is ___ on time. He is always at least five minutes late!

   a. sometimes

   b. usually

   c. never

   d. always

5. Jane and Cary are going to Europe this summer. Their parents ___ to learn more about the world before they go to college.

   a. wants their

   b. want their

   c. wants them

   d. want them

6. This spoon is dirty. Hand me ___ .

   a. other one next to coffeepot

   b. one next to the coffeepot

   c. another one next to coffeepot

   d. the other one next to the coffeepot

7. Barbara's exam scores are ___ April's exam scores.

   a. better than

   b. better

   c. more good than

   d. gooder than

8. You ___ your heavy coat to work. It's going to snow.

   a. might to take

   b. had better take

   c. could to take

   d. can take

Part 2. Error Identification. For questions 9 through 15, read each sentence carefully. Look at the underlined parts. Circle the letter that shows the incorrect part.

9. The democratic political system <u>have</u> <u>many benefits</u>, but drawbacks <u>exist</u> in <u>the</u>
                                            A   B   C   D

system, too.

10. The <u>roast beef</u> is <u>most</u> ready. It just <u>needs</u> to cook for ten <u>more</u> minutes.
          A   B   C   D

11. The state representatives <u>are going</u> to <u>vote</u> on the new tax bill before <u>the end of</u> this
                                  A   B   C

<u>year</u> legislative session.
D

12. The stockholders <u>might</u> definitely <u>sell their</u> shares, <u>or they</u> will lose all of the capital
                          A   B   C

that <u>they have invested in the company so far.</u>
                          D

13. The <u>house the prime minister</u>, which is <u>in</u> a very nice section <u>of town</u>, is visited by
                       A   B   C

countless <u>tourists</u> every year.
          D

14. The Census Bureau <u>sended</u> out over two <u>million copies</u> of that form to <u>families</u> in
                        A   B   C

every state <u>in</u> the country.
              D

15. <u>Many people</u> believe <u>that best</u> artisan <u>crafts</u> can be found in the countries located <u>in</u>
    A   B   C   D

northern Africa.

Unit 2

Phrasal Verbs

Exercise 1.   **Realia** Read the following mystery story. Underline the seven phrasal verbs. If there is a pronoun object, underline it, too.

The Alaska Mystery

It was another working day for the Alaska detective. The police called him up and asked him to find out information about a suspicious December death. The detective heard a low voice coming from the back bedroom. He knew something was not right, so he walked toward that room and slowly unlocked the door. The sound he heard was coming from a radio near the door. The detective quickly turned it off. It was cold in the room, so he put on his old tan raincoat. In the center of the room he saw a woman lying on the floor. He cautiously approached her and examined her dead body. She was on her back, and her right hand was clenched on top of her chest. Under her hand was a deep wound, similar to the wound a knife would make. He looked at the items in the room again. How did she die? Where was the weapon? He couldn't figure it out. There was nothing in the room except the radio near the door and a pool of water on the floor under the woman. It was impossible for someone to enter the house because every door and every window were locked. This was not an easy case, but the detective was very smart. He began to sweat. He took off his raincoat and investigated more. He was sure it wasn't a homicide. Did she kill herself? He looked at the woman and the water again. All at once he took out his notebook and began to write. Eureka! He had the answer!

Exercise 2.   **Original Sentence Writing** Read the following sentences. Imagine that you are the speaker. What will you say next? Write a comment that might follow each of the sentences below. Be sure to include a phrasal verb in your sentences. Underline the phrasal verbs. (*Hint:* You can use phrases such as *I need to* or *I have to* or *I should* in your comments.)

1. My bedroom is a mess!

_____

2. The fire is getting too big!

_____

3. I don't want anybody reading my private letter.

_____

4. My ears hurt. The music's too loud.

_____

5. I don't know the definition of this word.

_____

6. There's a twenty-dollar bill on the ground.

_____

7. I can never remember my cousin's telephone number.

_____

8. I wanted to have a party at my house next week, but I have to work that night.

_____

Exercise 3.   **Realia** Read Paul's list of things that he has to do today. Fill in the blanks with the appropriate particles.

> ### TO DO TODAY
>
> 1. Pick _____ Sam from soccer practice
> 2. Take _____ the garbage before tomorrow morning
> 3. Put _____ Sam's toys
> 4. Throw _____ the leftovers in the fridge
> 5. Give _____ the cake pan I borrowed from the Johnsons
> 6. Try _____ the new suit I bought yesterday
> 7. Call _____ George to ask about the car he's selling
> 8. Fill _____ the application for a new credit card

Exercise 4. **Puzzle/Game** Reread the first exercise in this unit. When you finish, read the note the woman left behind. In the note you will find some clues as to how she died. Underline the four phrasal verbs and then answer the questions below.

To all my loved ones,

I cannot get through another day. After this last heartbreak, I fear my heart will not get over the pain of my lost love. I used to get along with the love of my life, but he betrayed me. When I found out what he did, it felt like a knife piercing my heart. To that end, I decided I could not live anymore. The knife I use will be as icy as the feeling in my heart.

Good-bye, my friends.

Peace.

What we know from the scene (p. 10)

1. The woman lived in the state of _____ .

2. The season is _____ .

3. The only things in the room are the radio and the _____ by the body.

What we know from the note (p. 12)

The woman was betrayed.

4. The woman suffered from a broken _____ .

The woman used some kind of sharp object, similar to a knife.

5. Based on the information, how do you think the woman died?

_____

Exercise 5.   **Dialogue and Conversation Practice** Khalid and Ahmad haven't talked to each other in a long time. Write a dialogue between them (questions and answers) using at least six of the phrasal verbs below.

find out	make up	pick up	take off	turn on	come across
count on	get over	look after	run into	eat out	slow down

Khalid: _____

Ahmad: _____

Khalid: _____

Ahmad: _____

Khalid: _____

Ahmad: _____

Khalid: _____

Ahmad: _____

Khalid: _____

Ahmad: _____

Exercise 6.   **Sentence Study** Read the beginning sentences. Then read the answer choices and put a check mark in front of **all of the sentences that are true** based on the beginning sentences. Remember that more than one answer is possible sometimes.

1. The students asked their teacher, Mrs. Brown, to slow down.
   ___ a. She is always angry.
   ___ b. Her book doesn't have the correct answers.
   ___ c. Perhaps she talks too fast.
   ___ d. If Mrs. Brown slows down, the students will be happier.

2. Mary gave up after three weeks of working at her new job.
   ___ a. She quit her job.
   ___ b. She got a promotion.
   ___ c. She stayed at her new job for three weeks.
   ___ d. She left her new job three weeks ago.

3. As usual, flight 425 landed at 4:00 P.M., and the entire flight lasted only 50 minutes.
   ___ a. The plane arrived at 4:00 P.M.
   ___ b. The plane was delayed for almost an hour.
   ___ c. The plane took off at 4:50 P.M.
   ___ d. At 3:25 P.M., the flight was in the air.

4. The secretary wrote down a message for you and asked you to deal with it as soon as you can.
   ___ a. The secretary wants you to take care of the message as soon as possible.
   ___ b. Because she has a bad memory, the secretary made a note of the message for you.
   ___ c. The secretary didn't understand the contents of the message.
   ___ d. The secretary left a message for you.

5. Sally left out her name on the application.
   ___ a. She wrote her name on the top line of the application.
   ___ b. She wrote her entire name, but she made a mistake with the spelling.
   ___ c. She wrote her name on the left side of the application.
   ___ d. She forgot to write her name on the application.

6. When the teacher handed back the vocabulary exams, Bruce tore his paper up.
   ___ a. He was probably very happy with his grade.
   ___ b. His exam score wasn't very good.
   ___ c. He put the paper in his notebook so he could look at it later on.
   ___ d. It's impossible for him to look at his answers any more.

7. When I saw Joshua, he was trying on several pairs of basketball shoes.
   ___ a. This meeting probably took place at a shoe store.
   ___ b. This meeting probably took place at Joshua's house.
   ___ c. It is possible that Joshua bought some shoes.
   ___ d. Joshua wanted to see if the shoes were the correct size.

8. Lisa called me back two hours after I left the message on her phone at work at noon.
   ___ a. Lisa called me at 10 A.M.
   ___ b. I left a message for Lisa.
   ___ c. Lisa called me at 2 P.M.
   ___ d. I called Lisa first.

Exercise 7.   **TOEFL Review**

Part 1.   Completion. For items 1 through 8, circle the letter of the answer that best completes the statement or question.

1. __ that car! It's coming straight toward you!

   a. Go off

   b. Watch out for

   c. Look after

   d. Get through

2. The teacher __ the test answers for twenty minutes.

   a. gone over

   b. gone through

   c. went over

   d. went to

3. *Nancy:*   Did you __ an application?

   Joel: No, I'll do that tomorrow.

   a. called off

   b. picked up

   c. call off

   d. pick up

4. Can you look __ my dog while I'm on vacation?

   a. up

   b. over

   c. after

   d. through

5. Jill and Greg need to __ when the bus leaves.

   a. look over

   b. get into

   c. find out

   d. put away

6. Marsha is very responsible. You can always ___ .

    a. count her

    b. count on

    c. count her on

    d. count on her

7. The cookies are burning! Turn ___ the oven.

    a. off

    b. on

    c. away

    d. back

8. When I don't feel like cooking at home, I usually eat ___ .

    a. in

    b. over

    c. down

    d. out

Part 2. Error Identification. In items 9 through 15, read each sentence carefully. Look at the underlined parts. Circle the letter that shows the incorrect part.

9. Linda <u>didn't</u> find <u>out about</u> the <u>test</u> until <u>afternoon yesterday</u>.
        A   B   C   D

10. My <u>weekly</u> chore <u>is</u> to take <u>off</u> the garbage, but I'd prefer <u>a different chore</u>.
          A   B   C   D

11. I <u>called you</u> yesterday, but no one <u>were</u> home. <u>What</u> time did you <u>get in</u>?
         A   B   C   D

12. <u>The</u> bus <u>usually drops</u> the passengers <u>down</u> on the corner <u>of Elm</u> and Oak.
     A   B   C   D

13. Because <u>the</u> original notes were thrown <u>by</u>, the secretary <u>had to</u> retype <u>them</u> from
           A   B   C   D

    scratch.

14. <u>None of</u> the students <u>felt</u> prepared for the big <u>exam, so</u> the professor <u>put off</u> one
      A   B   C   D

    more day.

15. <u>She scheduled</u> a meeting, <u>but</u> she <u>had</u> to <u>call off it</u> suddenly.
        A   B   C   D

Unit 3

Past Progressive Tense

Exercise 1. **Realia** Look at the two schedules below. One is for Sarah MacNeal, and the other is for Ryan Brown. They both work at the same company. Use their schedules to answer the questions below. Write in complete sentences. Use *while* where necessary.

Sarah's Schedule

Monday, June 11	
9:00	Read Mail
10:00	
11:00	Meeting w/Mr. Green
12:00	Eat Lunch/Type Report
1:00	Meeting w/Supervisor
2:00	
3:00	
4:00	Return Phone Calls
5:00	Go to Gym
6:00	

Ryan's Schedule

Monday, June 11	
9:00	Call Clients
10:00	
11:00	Read Mail
12:00	Eat Lunch
1:00	Meeting w/Supervisor
2:00	Return Phone Calls/Write Memo
3:00	
4:00	Finish Financial Report
5:00	Pick Up Dog from Vet
6:00	

1. What was Sarah doing at 9:00 A.M.?

   _____

2. What was Ryan doing at 9:00 A.M.?

   _____

3. What was Sarah doing while Ryan was reading mail?

   _____

4. What else was Sarah doing while she was typing her report?

   _____

5. What were Sarah and Ryan doing at 1:00 P.M.?

   _____

6. What else was Ryan doing while he was returning phone calls?

_____

7. What was Ryan doing at 4:00 P.M.?

_____

8. What was Ryan doing while Sarah was at the gym?

_____

Exercise 2.   **Original Sentence Writing** Look in a magazine or newspaper to find a photo or drawing that has many actions taking place. Paste or attach your picture to the box below. Then write five sentences that describe what happened or was happening. Use *when* or *while.*

1. _____

2. _____

3. _____

4. _____

5. _____

Exercise 3. **Realia** Look at the following accident report from an insurance company. Use it to answer the questions below. Write in complete sentences. Use *when* or *while* when appropriate.

```
             Accident Report

Insured/Claimant: John Applewhite      Phone: (212) 555-1212

Date of Accident: September 22         Time: 5:30 ( ) AM (X) PM

Location: Corner of Broad Avenue and Eighth Street

Describe What Happened:
1. Mr. Applewhite was driving south on Broad Avenue at 5:25 P.M.
2. He stopped to make a left turn onto Eighth Street at 5:30 P.M.
3. The car behind him failed to stop.
4. The other car hit the back of Mr. Applewhite's car.
5. Mr. Applewhite got out of his car, but the other driver remained
   in his vehicle.
6. Mr. Applewhite called the police from his cellular phone. The
   other driver was talking to a passenger in his car.
7. The police gave the other driver a ticket for reckless driving.

Describe Damage to Vehicle:
         Rear bumper of vehicle destroyed. Rear tail lights broken.

Estimated Amount (if known): $700.00

Witnesses: Robert Steiner               Phone: 212-555-4235

Accident Reported By: John Applewhite    Date: September 22
```

1. What was Mr. Applewhite doing at 5:25 P.M.?

   _____

2. What happened to Mr. Applewhite when he stopped his car?

   _____

3. What happened when the other driver hit Mr. Applewhite's car?*

   _____

4. What was the other driver doing while Mr. Applewhite called the police?

   _____

5. When the police arrived, what did they do?

   _____

* In numbers 3 and 5, the use of *when* is equivalent to the meaning of *after*. If the time difference between two actions is very small, it is common to use *when* although technically the better (or more accurate) connecting word would be *after*.

Exercise 4. **Puzzle/Game** Read the riddle below. Write the correct progressive form of each verb listed below. When you are finished, write the letters that are circled on the numbered lines to reveal the answer to the riddle.

Riddle of the Sphinx

What walks on four legs in the morning,
Two legs in the afternoon, and
Three legs in the evening?

1. break   _ _ ◯ _ _ _ _

2. laugh   _ _ _ ◯ _ _ _

3. urge   ◯ _ _ _ _ _

4. hum   _ _ ◯ _ _ _

5. dance   _ ◯ _ _ _ _

6. run   _ _ ◯ _ _ _

7. pad   _ ◯ _ _ _ _

8. lose   _ ◯ _ _ _

9. enter   _ _ ◯ _ _ _ _

10. sew   ◯ _ _ _ _

The answer: ___ ___ ___ ___ ___ ___   ___ ___ ___ ___ .
                 1   2   3   4   5   6   7   8   9   10

Exercise 5. **Dialogue and Conversation Practice** Kathryn had a very exciting experience at the grocery store. She is telling Natasha about it. Fill in the blanks with the correct form of the verbs in parentheses. Use either past progressive tense or simple past tense.

Kathryn: You won't believe who I saw today!

Natasha: Who?

Kathryn: Mel Gibson!

Natasha: No way! Where did you see him?

Kathryn: You won't believe it. I **1** _____ (stand) in line at

the grocery store when he **2** _____ (walk) up

behind me.

Natasha: That's incredible! What **3** _____ (do) when you

4 _____ (see) him?

Kathryn: Well, I tried not to scream. I turned around and introduced myself.

Natasha: What **5** _____ (say) when you

6 _____ (do) that?

Kathryn: Actually, he was very nice to me. We had a nice conversation. It was great!

While we **7** _____ (talk), everybody

8 _____ (stare) at us.

Natasha: Wow! How exciting! Did you get his autograph?

Kathryn: Yes! After they rang up my food, I asked him to sign my receipt. He

9 _____ (sign) it while they

10 _____ (ring up) his food. Here it is!

Natasha: You are so lucky! It's too bad you didn't have a camera with you. You could

have gotten a picture with him.

Kathryn: I know, but I am happy that I got to meet him. I'll always remember it.

Exercise 6. **Sentence Study** Read the beginning sentences. Then read the answer choices and put a check mark in front of **all of the sentences that are true** based on the beginning sentences. Remember that more than one answer is possible sometimes.

1. While the children were studying, their uncle was making dinner.
   ___ a. First, their uncle made dinner. Then the children studied.
   ___ b. First, their children studied. Then the uncle made dinner.
   ___ c. The uncle made dinner. Their children studied at the same time.
   ___ d. After the children ate dinner, they studied.

2. I was playing tennis when I sprained my ankle.
   ___ a. First, I played tennis. Later, I sprained my ankle.
   ___ b. First, I sprained my ankle. Then I played tennis.
   ___ c. I played tennis. Afterward, I sprained my ankle.
   ___ d. I hurt my ankle during the tennis game.

3. While Jenny was sleeping, a burglar broke into her house.
   ___ a. First, the burglar broke into the house. Then Jenny went to sleep.
   ___ b. First, Jenny fell asleep. Then a burglar got into her house.
   ___ c. Jenny slept all night. After that, a burglar came into her house.
   ___ d. When the burglar came to the house, Jenny was asleep.

4. The little girl smiled when she saw the clown.
   ___ a. The girl was not happy to see the clown.
   ___ b. First, the girl smiled. Then she saw the clown.
   ___ c. The girl smiled because she saw the clown.
   ___ d. The girl frowned when she saw the clown.

5. They were standing in line when the cashier closed her register.
   ___ a. They were probably in some kind of store.
   ___ b. The cashier stopped working after they got in line.
   ___ c. They were waiting to buy something.
   ___ d. The cashier stopped working after they left the line.

6. Marsha read a book while she was waiting in line.
   ___ a. Marsha finished her book before she got in line.
   ___ b. Marsha wanted to read her book, but she couldn't.
   ___ c. Marsha got in line and started to read her book.
   ___ d. Marsha got in line to buy a book to read.

7. Peter said, "I can finish this homework while I eat dinner."
   ___ a. He probably doesn't need to use a computer for his homework.
   ___ b. He will eat dinner after he finishes his homework.
   ___ c. He will eat dinner and do his homework at the same time.
   ___ d. He plans to finish his homework and then eat his dinner.

8. The flight attendants on my recent flight from Toronto to Los Angeles talked to the passengers while they were serving them dinner.

___ a. The flight attendants chatted with the passengers while they were serving dinner.

___ b. The flight started in Toronto and ended in Los Angeles.

___ c. The flight attendants served dinner on the flight.

___ d. During the dinner service on the flight, the flight attendants talked with the passengers.

Exercise 7.   **TOEFL Review**

Part 1.   Completion. For items 1 through 8, circle the letter of the answer that best completes the statement.

1. Janice and Bill ___ when the phone rang.

   a. were ate dinner

   b. were eating dinner

   c. was ate the dinner

   d. was eating the dinner

2. The House of Representatives and the Senate approved the bill, but the president ___ it.

   a. vetoed

   b. was vetoing

   c. did vetoed

   d. was veto

3. Michael and I were both very busy yesterday at 6:00 P.M. While I was doing laundry, he ___ .

   a. were balancing the checkbook

   b. balance the checkbook

   c. was balancing the checkbook

   d. balanced checkbook

4. The audience members became incredibly enthusiastic when ___.

   a. arrive the guest speaker

   b. the guest speaker arrive

   c. arrived the guest speaker

   d. the guest speaker arrived

5. The children ___ to school when it started to rain.

   a. walking

   b. did walked

   c. were walking

   d. walked

6. Lucinda was doing her homework when Barbara suddenly ___ her if she could borrow one thousand dollars.

   a. asked

   b. asking

   c. was asking

   d. was ask

7. The dog barked ___.

   a. when rang the doorbell

   b. when the doorbell rang

   c. the doorbell when rang

   d. the doorbell rang

8. Arnold ___ when the lights went out, so of course he had to stop reading it.

   a. was reading the newspaper

   b. read the newspaper

   c. was reading newspaper

   d. read newspaper

Part 2. Error Identification. For items 9 through 15, read each sentence carefully. Look at the underlined parts. Circle the letter that shows the incorrect part of the sentence sequence.

9. Yesterday Mark and Greg were playing soccer in the park when it was starting to rain.
   A   B   C   D

10. Many dogs sitting by the door waiting until their owners arrive home from work.
             A   B   C   D

11. What you were doing when I called you last night?
   A   B   C   D

12. The chef burned her right hand badly while was frying some meat in the newly
                             A   B   C   D

remodeled kitchen.

13. While Mary was mowing lawn, Lisa was raking up leaves in the backyard.
   A   B   C   D

14. At around ten o'clock last night, the hotel's night auditor balancing the accounting
      A   B   C

books by himself.
      D

15. The doctor's notes on the prescription was illegible, so the pharmacist could not fill
   A   B

the prescription, and the patient did not receive any of the medication.
 C   D

Unit 4

Present Perfect Tense

Exercise 1. **Realia** The English School is conducting a survey to find out how people have learned English. You will participate in this survey by completing the questions below. Use sentences in the present perfect or present perfect progressive tenses.

Survey

1. How long have you been studying English? _____
   _____

2. Have you ever lived in an English-speaking country? If yes, where were you? _____
   And how long did you live there? _____

3. Has anybody else in your family studied English? _____ If yes, who? _____
   _____ How long did he or she study English? _____

4. Have you seen any English language movies? _____ Can you list the names of
   at least three movies that you saw in English? _____
   _____
   _____

5. What is the most important activity that has helped you improve your English? _____
   _____

Exercise 2. **Original Sentence Writing** For each item, you will write two sentences. For the first statement or question, use the words below. Be sure to use the present perfect tense. Underline the present perfect tense. Then write a sentence that might follow the first one in a conversation. The first one has been done for you.

1. Jack / gone / to that theater / many times

   Jack **has gone** to that theater many times.

   He says it's one of the best in this area.

2. you / drive / to Miami / before?

   _____

   _____

3. Mr. and Mrs. Volks / not live / here very long

   _____

   _____

4. you / feed / the cats / yet?

   _____

   _____

5. *Alex:*   Do you know where Mrs. Solomon is?

   Brad: No, I don't. I / be / in a meeting / for the last three hours.

   _____

   _____

6. *John:*   That's a beautiful blanket. Did you make it?

   Alice: Yes. I / take / knitting lessons / for the last three months.

   _____

   _____

7. *Jeanine:*   you / not water / those plants / yet?

   _____

   _____

   Keith: No, but I'll water them today. I promise!

8. *Edgar:*   you / go / to California / ever?

   _____

   _____

   Ikumi: Yes, I have. I went there last summer. It's beautiful!

Exercise 3. **Realia** Complete the postcard from Joanna to her parents using the present perfect tense.

Dear Mom and Dad,

I'm having a great time in New York City! It is ❶ _____ _____ (most / interesting city / I / ever / visit). I saw the Statue of Liberty yesterday, and I went to Chinatown today. I ❷ _____ _____ (not / be / to Broadway / yet), but I have tickets for a show tomorrow night. ❸ _____ _____ (I / be / to a lot of restaurants). I won't be hungry for a long time! I will be home on Friday. ❹ _____ _____ (you / be / to the Metropolitan Museum / ever)? This is the first time ❺ _____ _____ _____ (I / go / there). I'll see you on Friday!

Love, Joanna

Exercise 4. **Puzzle/Game** Read the clues for the crossword puzzle. Then fill in the answers in the puzzle.

Across

2. Have you _____ the news? Joe is getting married.

3. Nicole has _____ that movie three times this week!

4. Josephine went to New York _____ year.

6. The past participle of *write* is _____ .

8. Mary has _____ to him on the phone many times.

Down

1. I have been studying _____ three hours.

2. You _____ been to that movie yet? I don't believe it!

5. How long has it been _____ you have seen him?

6. When you were in Japan, did you _____ a kimono?

7. I have _____ been there for a long time. Maybe I'll go next year.

Exercise 5.   **Dialogue and Conversation Practice** Sherry and Melissa are very good friends. They haven't seen each other in a long time. Write a dialogue between them using as many of the following vocabulary items as possible.

dating	travel	children	so far	since _____
mother	money	job/work	ever	for _____

_____

_____

_____

_____

_____

_____

_____

_____

_____

_____

Exercise 6. **Sentence Study** Read the beginning sentences. Then read the answer choices and put a check mark in front of **all of the sentences that are true** based on the beginning sentences. Remember that more than one answer is possible sometimes.

1. *Charlie:* I haven't finished packing my suitcase yet! I'm going to be late!
   Sara: Don't worry. I've just finished packing. I'll help you.
   ___ a. Charlie's problem is that he has too many things in his suitcase.
   ___ b. Sara probably packed her suitcase several hours ago.
   ___ c. Charlie isn't ready to go yet.
   ___ d. Sara has offered to help Charlie with his suitcase.

2. *Joe:* How much money have you spent on presents?
   Jake: I started out with $300, and I've spent about $175 so far.
   ___ a. Jake doesn't have any money left.
   ___ b. Jake has $175 left.
   ___ c. Jake has about $125 left.
   ___ d. Jake didn't spend enough money.

3. *Gina:* How long have you lived in Korea?
   Kristan: I have lived here for 10 years.
   ___ a. Kristan doesn't live in Korea, but she did.
   ___ b. Kristan was in Korea 10 years ago.
   ___ c. Kristan still lives in Korea.
   ___ d. Kristan has been in Korea for 10 years.

4. *Andrew:* I have read three books this semester. I have also turned in three book reports. I still have to read five more books and write reports for them before the end of the semester.
   Sandra: That's incredible!
   ___ a. Sandra is amazed at the amount of work that Andrew is doing.
   ___ b. Andrew already wrote three book reports.
   ___ c. Andrew has to write a report for each book that he has to read.
   ___ d. The total number of reports that Andrew has to write is eight.

5. *Maggie:* How many times have you tried to call the electric company?
   Coleen: This is the fifth time I have called that office. They still haven't picked up the phone!
   ___ a. Coleen has called the electric company several times.
   ___ b. Coleen has talked to someone who works at the electric company.
   ___ c. When she called the electric company, no one answered.
   ___ d. The person who answered the telephone at the electric company was rude.

6. *Mohammed:* Mark has finished his homework already.

    Alisha: Wow, I haven't even started mine yet. What about you?

    Mohammed: I have done four exercises, but I still have three more to do.

    ___ a. None of them has done any of the homework.

    ___ b. The homework assignment consists of seven exercises.

    ___ c. Mohammed has finished four exercises.

    ___ d. Mohammed has done more homework than Alisha.

7. *David:* Did you send in your job application?

    Jim: Thanks for asking. I've just sent it!

    ___ a. David mailed Jim's application for him.

    ___ b. Jim sent his application a little while ago.

    ___ c. David asked about Jim's application.

    ___ d. Jim mailed his application while he was talking to David.

8. *Joyce:* What is your favorite roller coaster?

    George: Montu at Busch Gardens in Florida. I have ridden on it fifteen times so far.

    Joyce: My favorite is Gwazi, but I have only ridden on it two times.

    ___ a. Joyce has been on Gwazi many times.

    ___ b. George has been on Gwazi many times.

    ___ c. Joyce has been on Montu many times.

    ___ d. George has been on Montu many times.

Exercise 7.   **TOEFL Review**

Part 1. Completion. For items 1 through 8, circle the letter of the answer that best completes the statement or question.

1. She ___ in three weeks.

    a. has gone to work

    b. went to the work

    c. hasn't gone to work

    d. goes to the work

2. William ___ soccer many times before.

    a. has played

    b. have played

    c. has play

    d. have play

3. ___ to you yet?

    a. Did Valentina spoken

    b. Is Valentina speak

    c. Has Valentina spoken

    d. Did Valentina spoke

4. The band ___ here many times.

    a. is playing

    b. has played

    c. have played

    d. play

5. ___ here before? It looks familiar.

    a. Hasn't we been

    b. Aren't we

    c. Didn't we

    d. Haven't we been

6. The director of the film ___ . He's really looking forward to seeing it.

    a. have seen the final cut yet

    b. hasn't seen the final cut yet

    c. haven't seen already the final cut

    d. hasn't seen already the final cut

7. The party guests ___ . They aren't hungry anymore.

    a. haven't eaten yet

    b. have just eaten

    c. are eaten already

    d. be eating now

8. How long ___ at the university?

   a. have Dr. Jones taught geology

   b. have Dr. Jones taught the geology

   c. has Dr. Jones taught geology

   d. has Dr. Jones taught the geology

Part 2. Error Identification. For items 9 through 15, read each sentence carefully. Look at the underlined parts. Circle the letter that shows the incorrect part of the sentence.

9. <u>Neither my cousin nor</u> I <u>have</u> been to that movie <u>already</u> because she's been ill lately
       A   B   C

   <u>and I've been</u> busy.
      D

10. The <u>children</u> playing in the house <u>aren't</u> had any pumpkin pie <u>yet</u> because it's <u>still</u> in
       A   B   C   D

   the oven.

11. The supervisor <u>have</u> given the employee three <u>warnings</u> up till <u>now</u>, but the
              A   B   C

   <u>employee's attitude and actions have not changed at all</u>.
                   D

12. My wife <u>and</u> I <u>have been</u> to that theater many <u>times</u> when <u>we lived</u> in Tampa.
         A   B   C   D

13. <u>Extremely unhappy</u> with the government's decision to raise taxes, in 1973 Henry
     A

   Jackson <u>has organized</u> a group <u>of citizens</u> in protest <u>against</u> the government.
            B   C   D

14. Oliver <u>has</u> lived in <u>Seattle, largest</u> city <u>in</u> Washington, <u>for</u> three years.
       A   B   C   D

15. Jimmy <u>Carter, a former</u> peanut farmer, <u>lived</u> in <u>the</u> White House <u>during</u>
         A   B   C   D

   four years.

Unit 5
Adverbs of Manner
and Related Terms

Exercise 1. **Realia** Read this incredible advertisement for an amazing new product that can help students who are trying to learn English. Underline the nine adverbs in the advertisement.

Dr. Smith's English Pills

Are you tired of studying hard for exams and not doing well? Try Dr. Smith's English Pills. They really work! With Dr. Smith's English Pills, all you need is one small tablet in the morning. By taking this pill, you will learn English more quickly and easily. Here's how it works...

The special formula in Dr. Smith's Pills uses a unique enzyme that stimulates the part of the brain used for learning languages. When this part of the brain is activated, language abilities automatically increase!

Here's what one user of Dr. Smith's English Pills says about the product.

"I can't believe it. I started taking the English pills three weeks ago, and now I can speak clearly and fluently in English. I recommend Dr. Smith's Pills wholeheartedly. Now that's a word I would have never used two months ago! Try them. They work!"

J. A., English language student, Boston, Massachusetts

For more information about Dr. Smith's English Pills, call 1-800-000-0000. You'll be amazed at the results.

Exercise 2.   **Original Sentence Writing** Read the following sentences. Change the form of each sentence to include an adverb instead of an adjective. Then add a second sentence that might follow the first one in a conversation. The first one has been done for you.

1. Barbara is a quick notetaker.

    Barbara takes notes quickly.

    She does well on the tests because her notes are so good.

2. The teacher told us to be punctual to class.

    _____

    _____

3. Lucia thought the answers to the test questions were easy.

    _____

    _____

4. Bobby looked happy as he left school.

    _____

    _____

5. The schoolchildren are careful when they cross the street.

    _____

    _____

6. Maryanne was silent as she received the doctor's evaluation.

    _____

    _____

7. Louise is an excellent boxer.

    _____

    _____

8. The painters did a poor job repainting our home.

    _____

    _____

Exercise 3. **Realia** Read this e-mail response from Lucinda to her sister Joanne. Circle the correct form of the words in parentheses.

```
Date: Mon., 6 November 2000 8:05:45 -0400 (EDT)
From: Lucky@lifenet.com
To:     Jojo@gorgon.net
Subject: Here's what I think

Hello JoJo:

I'm sorry to hear about all the problems you've been having. Here's what
I think you should do.  You can take my advice or not . . . but let me
know how things turn out. First, you should talk to Billy ❶ (with a, by)
phone because it will be much more personal than expressing yourself
❷ (by writing, with writing) a letter.  In your conversation, I think you
should ask him if he is serious about ending the friendship. ❸ (By don't,
By not) saying anything, you will never know what he is feeling.  You
should also let him know that you were unaware of his feelings. ❹ (With,
By) being honest, you will feel better, regardless of the final outcome.


You have been going out with Billy for a long time, and I'm sure that ❺
(by, with) a little bit of patience, your relationship will become strong
again. It doesn't help that you are both living in different cities.
You know, miscommunications can happen, and ❻ (by, with) talking to him
as soon as possible, you will get the information you need.

Good luck to you, and be sure to contact me soon, preferably ❼ (by, with
an) e-mail, to let me know what happens.  I love you, and I hope to hear
from you soon.

Your sister,
Lucinda


P.S.  Have you heard that Joey will be coming to visit me this summer ❽
(by, with a) boat?  He'll finally get to show off the great new sailboat
he bought!
```

Exercise 4. **Puzzle/Game** Read the sentences below. In each sentence, fill in the correct —*ing* verb that answers the question *how?* Then use the letters in the circles to answer the puzzle question below.

1. You can improve your English by __ __ __ __ __ _Ⓞ_ __ __ with native speakers.

2. You can become healthier by __ __ __ Ⓞ __ __ __ __ __ __ at the gym.

3. You can make new friends by __ Ⓞ __ __ __ __ __ a club or group.

4. You can maintain good grades by __ __ __ Ⓞ __ all your homework.

5. You can have a nice smile by __ __ __ __ __ Ⓞ __ __ your teeth every day.

6. You can learn to cook by __ __ __ __ Ⓞ __ a cooking class.

7. You can learn about different cultures by __ __ __ __ __ __ __ Ⓞ foreign

movies.

How can you make your shirts look neat and clean?

by __ __ __ __ __ __ __ them.

Exercise 5.   **Dialogue and Conversation Practice** Louise ran into Anna at the mall and was shocked! Anna had changed so much! Here are some of the changes that Louise noticed.

Anna Before	Anna Now
overweight	thin
gray hair	blonde hair
blue eyes	green eyes

Write a dialogue between Louise and Anna, with Louise asking questions about Anna's appearance.

Louise: Wow, Anna, you look great! _____

Anna: _____

Louise: _____

Anna: _____

Louise: _____

Anna: _____

Louise: _____

Anna: _____

Louise: _____

Anna: _____

Exercise 6.   **Sentence Study** Read the beginning sentences for questions 1 through 4. Then read the answer choices and put a check mark in front of all of the sentences that are true based on the beginning sentences. For questions 5 through 8, read the beginning questions. Then put a check mark in front of **all the answers that are possible** for the questions. Remember that more than one answer is possible sometimes.

1. Liz hardly studied for the test, and her test score showed this.
   ___ a. She was very prepared for the test.
   ___ b. She studied a lot for the exam.
   ___ c. Her test score probably wasn't very good.
   ___ d. Her test score was very different from what we expected.

2. They are good singers, but they can't write songs well.
   ___ a. They sing well.
   ___ b. They are good songwriters.
   ___ c. They rarely sing.
   ___ d. They don't write songs well.

3. Georgina types very accurately but not quickly.
   ___ a. She types often, but she can't type quickly.
   ___ b. She doesn't make many mistakes when she types.
   ___ c. She types quickly and accurately.
   ___ d. She is not a fast typist.

4. Instead of following her usual routine, Vicky traveled by plane
   on her business trip to Toronto last week.
   ___ a. Vicky's trip last week was for business purposes.
   ___ b. Vicky flew to Toronto last week.
   ___ c. Vicky doesn't usually travel by plane when she goes on business trips.
   ___ d. Vicky has a new job that requires her to travel a lot.

5. How did you learn to ski so well?
   ___ a. To live in the Alps. It was necessary for this kind of life.
   ___ b. By living in the Alps. We were able to ski most of the year.
   ___ c. To ski every day. It's a fact of life here.
   ___ d. From my father. He taught me when I was very young.

6. How will Lisa be able to afford her new car?
   ___ a. To get an extra part-time job.
   ___ b. In order to get an extra part-time job.
   ___ c. By getting an extra part-time job.
   ___ d. With the money from her new part-time job.

7. How can you lose weight permanently?
   ___ a. In order to do this, you have to eat more vegetables and fewer fatty foods.
   ___ b. It's not so complicated—you have to change your lifestyle.
   ___ c. By changing your lifestyle, you can lose weight permanently.
   ___ d. One way to accomplish this is by eating more vegetables and fewer
        fatty foods.

8. How did you finish cleaning the house so quickly?
   ___ a. I got some help from my friends.
   ___ b. To prepare for the party.
   ___ c. By asking my roommate to give me a hand.
   ___ d. In order to ask for some help from my roommate.

Exercise 7. TOEFL Review

Part 1. Completion. For items 1 through 8, circle the letter of the answer that best completes the statement or question.

1. Gerardo is an excellent singer with ___ .

   a. a wonderfully voice

   b. a wonderful voice

   c. a voice that is wonderfully

   d. a voice wonderful

2. Jerry got to his doctor's appointment ___ .

   a. with a taxi

   b. by taxi

   c. by take a taxi

   d. with taking a taxi

3. The students learned the grammar rules ___ .

   a. to study every day

   b. by studying every day

   c. with studying every day

   d. study every day

4. Did the twins go to the movies ___ ?

   a. by their mother

   b. mother

   c. with their mother

   d. to their mother

5. Roberto can speak English and ___ .

   a. fluently

   b. Italian with fluent

   c. Italian fluent

   d. Italian fluently

6. ___ every day, you can stay in shape.

   a. By exercise

   b. By exercising

   c. With exercising

   d. With exercise

7. In order ___ , she went to night school to learn about computer programming.

   a. get a better job

   b. to get a better job

   c. getting a better job

   d. gotten a better job

8. Henry improved his eyesight ___ glasses.

   a. and get

   b. get

   c. by getting

   d. with getting

Part 2. Error Identification. For items 9 through 15, read each sentence carefully. Look at the underlined parts. Circle the letter that shows the incorrect part of the sentence.

9. In order <u>be</u> on time <u>to class</u>, I must <u>wake up</u> at 7:00 A.M. <u>every day</u>.
         A   B   C   D

10. <u>The</u> girls <u>careless</u> left the iron on <u>in the</u> laundry room, so they had to come home
     A   B   C

    <u>to turn</u> it off.
     D

11. Many <u>people say</u> that the <u>best</u> way <u>to stay</u> healthy is to exercise <u>by</u> friends.
           A   B   C   D

12. She <u>doesn't</u> act very <u>good</u>, but her <u>speaking</u> voice is <u>beautiful</u>.
           A   B   C   D

13. The man <u>furiously</u> threw the menu <u>on the floor</u> when the waiter <u>didn't</u> come back
             A   B   C

    <u>to table</u>.
     D

14. <u>The</u> bank president <u>thoughtless</u> announced <u>the company</u> merger <u>by</u> e-mail.
    A   B   C   D

15. <u>Unlike</u> most of her friends, Susan <u>paid</u> for <u>her college</u> tuition <u>by her</u> credit card.
    A   B   C   D

Unit 6

Prepositions after Verbs and Adjectives

Exercise 1. **Realia** Below are three newspaper articles. Only one of the articles is true. First, fill in the blanks with the correct prepositions. Then, circle the title of the article you believe is true. Discuss your choice with a classmate.

Cheeseburgers Make Man Famous

Yesterday in Kenosha, Wisconsin, Boyd Randall became famous **①** _____ eating the most cheeseburgers at one time. Randall, a university student, ate more than three hundred cheeseburgers at a contest at a local restaurant. When asked why he decided to eat so much, he replied, "I am not taking any classes right now, and I was bored **②** _____ doing nothing. The contest gave me something to look forward **③** _____." Randall says that he didn't do anything special to prepare for the contest. He just ate his mom's good cooking, and that was enough. When asked for her opinion about her son's achievement, Randall's mother said that she was proud **④** _____ what her son had done.

Angry Alligator Keeps Woman from Work

Mary Hankins lives in Baton Rouge, Louisiana. Two days ago, Mary forgot to close her garage door. When she woke up the next morning, she found an alligator in her garage! She had to call her boss to explain her unusual predicament. "I can't come to work today," she told him. "I rely **⑤** _____ my car to get me to work, and today I found an alligator on the hood of my car!" Her boss understood why she was afraid **⑥** _____ getting in her car. Then Mary spoke **⑦** _____ an officer at Animal Control and asked **⑧** _____ help. After three hours of hard work, they caught the alligator and took the ferocious animal away.

Good Deed Is Rewarded

Angela Roberts is an unemployed waitress who lives in San Francisco, California. Yesterday, while she was waiting **⑨** _____ a bus, Angela found a wallet. Inside she found $100,000! However, instead of keeping the money for herself, Angela gave the wallet **⑩** _____ the police, who later returned it to Bill Bailey, the owner. Mr. Bailey was surprised **⑪** _____ Angela's decision to return the wallet. "When I talked **⑫** _____ the police about losing my wallet, they told me that I probably wouldn't get it back. I am so happy **⑬** _____ the finder's decision." This morning, Mr. Bailey plans to give Angela $1,000 as a reward for her help.

Exercise 2. **Original Sentence Writing** Answer each of the following questions using a complete sentence.

1. How long have you been interested in learning English?

_____

2. Have you ever been married?

_____

3. What is one thing that you are afraid of?

_____

4. What is one thing that you have complained about?

_____

5. What is one thing that you look at every day?

_____

6. What is one thing that you are crazy about?

_____

7. What is one thing you are fed up with?

_____

8. What is one thing that you have concentrated on recently?

_____

Exercise 3.   **Realia** Julia went to Paris on vacation. Read the postcard that she sent her mother. There are seven mistakes with prepositions. Find and correct them.

Dear Mom,

Wow! I am so excited on being in Paris. Everything is so beautiful. Lots of things have happened about me since I arrived. I have visited many interesting places and eaten lots of great food. I even got to talk for a famous French actor! I can find nothing to complain with. The only problem I have had was becoming accustomed for using the metro system. The first few times I used it, I had to ask to someone for help. Now I can go anywhere I want with no problems.

Thank you to letting me come on this trip. I love you! See you in August!

Yours,

Julia

Exercise 4. **Puzzle/Game** Write the correct preposition next to the words in the maze below. Then find the path through the maze. Once you have found your way through the maze, write one sentence for each set of words that your path crosses. You will have seven sentences in all. The first sentence is done for you.

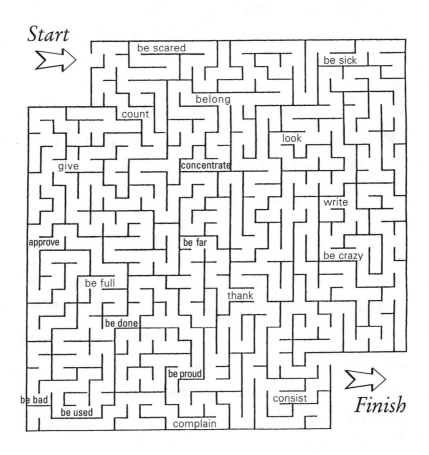

1. **I can always count on Mishal to do his homework.** _____

2. _____

3. _____

4. _____

5. _____

6. _____

7. _____

Exercise 5. **Dialogue and Conversation Practice** Frank's boss needs some information about the photocopy machine. Complete each sentence by writing the correct form of the word in parentheses and then adding the correct preposition. Remember that sometimes you will have to add the correct form of the verb *be* if the word in parentheses is an adjective.

Mr. Pruitt: Frank, I need to ❶ (talk) _____ you for a moment.

Frank: Okay, Mr. Pruitt. How can I help you?

Mr. Pruitt: I ❷ (aware) _____ the fact that the photocopy machine is not working. Can you tell me what ❸ (happen) _____ it?

Frank: The one on the first floor?

Mr. Pruitt: Yes.

Frank: That machine ❹ (famous) _____ always breaking down. I am afraid that it is so old that we just can't ❺ (depend) _____ it any longer. I think that we need to replace it.

Mr. Pruitt: I don't know if we can afford it. I will have to ask someone in the accounting department to ❻ (look) _____ some extra funds to pay for a new one.

Frank: If I ❼ (think) _____ a way to find the extra money, I will let you know.

Mr. Pruitt: Thanks, Frank. I'll talk with you later.

Frank: Okay. Good-bye.

Exercise 6. **Sentence Study** Read the beginning sentences. Then read the answer choices and put a check mark in front of **all of the sentences that are true** based on the beginning sentences. Remember that more than one answer is possible sometimes.

1. Donna and Curt are sick of hearing the same old excuses from their children about why they are getting bad grades in school.
   ___ a. Their children always use the same excuses.
   ___ b. Donna and Curt are ill.
   ___ c. The children aren't doing well in school.
   ___ d. The children are giving excuses about their grades to their parents.

2. These expensive silk ballet slippers belong to Andrea, who is an excellent ballet dancer.
   ___ a. Andrea is a ballet dancer.
   ___ b. The shoes cost a lot of money.
   ___ c. Andrea is wearing the slippers right now.
   ___ d. Andrea's slippers are made of silk.

3. Michael is never happy about anything. He always complains about everything.
   ___ a. Michael is difficult to please.
   ___ b. Michael is easy to please.
   ___ c. Because he isn't happy about anything, Michael complains a lot.
   ___ d. Basically, Michael is a happy man, but right now he's complaining about things.

4. I have laryngitis and cannot speak to you very loudly because it hurts when I talk. However, if you are quiet, you will be able to hear everything that I say.
   ___ a. You don't have to be quiet.
   ___ b. I am able to speak in a normal tone of voice.
   ___ c. It is difficult for me to speak.
   ___ d. You can talk as much as you want.

5. Paul is very angry at Lonnie. Lonnie forgot to pick him up from work last night.
   ___ a. Paul is not happy with Lonnie.
   ___ b. Paul forgot to get Lonnie from work.
   ___ c. Lonnie was supposed to meet Paul after work.
   ___ d. Lonnie forgot to do something for Paul.

6. We were very disappointed with the movie that we just saw. All of our friends said that it was really good, but we hated it.
   ___ a. Our friends liked the movie.
   ___ b. Not everyone liked the movie.
   ___ c. We went to a movie.
   ___ d. Our friends said that it was a good movie, but we didn't enjoy it very much.

7. My brother is so bad at sports that he rarely plays them. Whenever he does play, he hurts himself.
   ___ a. My brother hardly ever plays sports.
   ___ b. It is clear that my brother is a good athlete.
   ___ c. My brother often hurts himself when he plays sports.
   ___ d. My brother plays sports all the time, but he is not so good at them.

8. In grammar class, Lorenzo is studying the simple past tense, but he is confused by all the irregular verb forms.

___ a. Lorenzo has a grammar class.

___ b. Lorenzo understands well what he is studying in this class.

___ c. Irregular verb forms are not so easy for Lorenzo to understand.

___ d. Lorenzo is having problems with irregular verb forms, but he is not having problems with the irregular verb forms for the simple past tense.

Exercise 7. **TOEFL Review**

Part 1. Completion. For items 1 through 8, circle the letter of the answer that best completes the statement.

1. I don't like Don. He never agrees ___ anything that I say.

   a. of

   b. for

   c. with

   d. about

2. Don't forget ___ your grandma for the nice present.

   a. to think

   b. to approve

   c. to thank

   d. to give

3. Janet and Bill ___ waiting for us by the elevator at five o'clock.

   a. will

   b. will are

   c. are be

   d. will be

4. The children are ___ to going trick or treating on Halloween.

   a. thinking

   b. not forgetting

   c. waiting

   d. looking forward

5. The students are not very excited __ final exam.

   a. about take the

   b. about taking the

   c. about take

   d. about taking

6. Reynaldo isn't __ with his grades in grammar class. He thinks he needs to study more.

   a. crazy

   b. curious

   c. satisfied

   d. excited

7. My grandparents __ to rock music. They only listen to classical music.

   a. aren't used to listening

   b. used to listen

   c. are used to listening

   d. didn't used to listen

8. The beach is not __ here. Let's walk. It won't take us long at all.

   a. good at

   b. far from

   c. bad at

   d. similar to

Part 2. Error Identification. For items 9 through 15, read each sentence carefully. Look at the underlined parts. Circle the letter that shows the incorrect part of the sentence.

9. The children <u>are</u> not used to <u>play</u> so much during <u>the</u> day, which is why they get
          A   B   C

   <u>tired so quickly</u>.
      D

10. The <u>manager is</u> responsible <u>for</u> any <u>accidents</u> that occur <u>on</u> the restaurant.
           A   B   C   D

11. <u>How you</u> different <u>from</u> your <u>brothers</u> and <u>sisters</u>?
      A   B   C   D

12. I <u>need to</u> <u>concentrate for</u> my <u>studies, or</u> I <u>will fail</u> this semester.
     A   B   C   D

13. The mayor <u>wrote on</u> his congressperson <u>about</u> his <u>disappointment with</u> the <u>recently</u>
              A   B   C   D

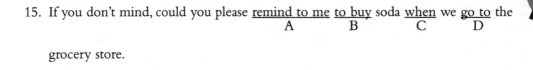

increased taxes.

14 <u>You can</u> <u>count in me</u> to help you <u>move to</u> your new <u>apartment next month</u>.
   A   B   C   D

15. If you don't mind, could you please <u>remind to me</u> <u>to buy</u> soda <u>when</u> we <u>go to</u> the
                                       A   B   C   D

grocery store.

Unit 7

Passive Voice

Realia Read the airline instructions below. Answer the questions using the active voice.

Welcome to *InterAir.*
For your safety
and comfort, please read the
instructions below:

1. Your seat must be kept in an upright and locked position for takeoff and landing.
2. Your seatbelt must be fastened at all times.
3. Carry-on baggage must be stored underneath your seat or in the overhead compartments.
4. Your meal will be served by the flight attendants once we reach cruising altitude.
5. The movie *You've Got Mail* will be played after your meal has been served.
6. Upon reaching our destination, your luggage may be picked up in the baggage claim area.

If you need any assistance during the flight, a flight attendant may be called by pushing the button above your head.

1. What must be done to your seatbelt?_____

_____

2. Where is carry-on baggage stored? _____

_____

3. Which film will the flight attendants show after the meal? _____

_____

4. Where will you find your luggage when you get off the plane? _____

_____

5. How can you call a flight attendant? _____

_____

6. When will your meal be served? _____

_____

Exercise 2.   **Original Sentence Writing** For each item, you will write two sentences. For the first statement or question, use the words below. Be sure to use the passive voice. Underline the passive voice. Then write a sentence that might follow the first one in a conversation. The first one has been done for you.

1. The Eiffel Tower / build / Alexandre-Gustave Eiffel

   The Eiffel Tower was built by Alexandre-Gustave Eiffel.

   I've never seen the Eiffel Tower, but one day I hope to see it.

2. The part of James Bond / play / Pierce Brosnan

   _____

   _____

3. How many / plays / write / William Shakespeare?

   _____

   _____

4. The computer / design / for children.

   _____

   _____

5. The assembly line / first / use / in Henry Ford's factory

   _____

   _____

6. Katy / embarrass / when she fell down the stairs

   _____

   _____

7. We / surprise / the end of the movie

   _____

   _____

8. When / the famous cathedral / complete?

_____

_____

Exercise 3.   **Realia** Read the movie review below. There are many verbs in the passive voice. On the lines under the review, rewrite the movie review using the active voice.

Passive Voice

Movie Corner

To Die Now by Phil M. Viewer

Last night I saw a movie that must be seen by everyone in the nation! The lead roles of Julianna and Rolf are played beautifully by Nikki Coleman and Red Manly. Julianna is kidnapped by a neighbor, and Rolf is assigned to her case. Frantic, Julianna's mother is overcome with grief and is unable to assist Rolf in his pursuit of her beloved daughter. Surprising twists and turns make the movie believable. If you want to know the ending, ask to be taken to this movie. It is a must see! Four stars!

★★★★

Active Voice

_____

_____

_____

_____

_____

_____

_____

_____

_____

Exercise 4.   **Puzzle/Game** Read the clues for the crossword puzzle. Then fill in the answers in the puzzle.

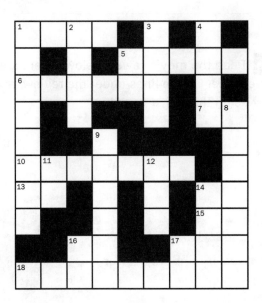

Across

1. The director is very satisfied _____ the new teacher.

5. I am so _____ with reading the same kinds of books every day!

6. Have you _____ to Susan about the party on Saturday?

7. Is *gave* the past participle for the verb *give?*

10. Are you going to be _____ by relatives from out of town this weekend?

13. These are two letters that are frequently found at the end of irregular past participles.

14. Are you used _____ being so late?

Down

1. The child _____ _____ a new toy for her birthday. (2 words)

2. "The photo was taken by Jill" is the same as "Jill _____ the photo."

3. Are you _____ with your homework now? If so, let's go to the mall!

4. Have you ever _____ on a 747?

5. What time will you _____ back home tonight?

8. A very small number of the students are _____ to this plan, but most of the others agree.

9. Driving from sunrise to sunset can be one of the most _____ things a human can do!

Across

15. The number one player on our soccer team _____ considered to be one of the best players in the whole state.

16. Are you interested _____ going to a movie with me later?

17. Most of the people here _____ worried about their English skills.

18. Many of the parents were _____ when they saw how much violence the movie had.

Down

11. I couldn't stay long at Mark's house because I was _____ a hurry to get home.

12. "Millions of hamburgers are eaten every day" means the same as "People _____ millions of hamburgers every day."

14. What verb do the adjectives *tired* and *tiring* come from?

16. Going to the Atlantic Ocean beaches _____ an exciting trip.

17. I like basketball a lot, and I play it once or twice a week. However, I'm not very good _____ it.

▬▬▬▬

Exercise 5.   **Dialogue and Conversation Practice** You are a driving instructor. Give instructions to a group of students who are learning how to drive.

Try to use both the passive and the active voice. Draw one line under any active voice verbs and two lines under any passive voice verbs. Use some of the vocabulary below.

ignition	key	break	mirror	seatbelt	fasten
forward	drive	must	should	adjust	reverse

_____

_____

_____

_____

_____

_____

_____

Exercise 6. **Sentence Study** Read the beginning sentences. Then read the answer choices and put a check mark in front of **all of the sentences that are true** based on the beginning sentences. Remember that more than one answer is possible sometimes.

1. Mr. Smith's house was built in 1949, so it's over fifty years old.
   ___ a. Mr. Smith built his house over fifty years ago.
   ___ b. Mr. Smith was born in 1949.
   ___ c. The house was built before Mr. Smith was born.
   ___ d. Mr. Smith's house is at least fifty-one years old.

2. Vegetarians are opposed to eating meat, and some vegetarians won't eat any dairy products such as cheese or yogurt either.
   ___ a. All vegetarians do not eat cheese.
   ___ b. Vegetables are permitted in vegetarians' diets but not meat.
   ___ c. Yogurt is not permitted in some vegetarians' diets.
   ___ d. Vegetarians do not eat meat.

3. When the teacher announced the results of last Tuesday's test, it was obvious that he was disappointed in his students' results.
   ___ a. The teacher was not satisfied with the students' test scores.
   ___ b. The teacher wished that the students' grades were higher.
   ___ c. The test was last Tuesday.
   ___ d. The students probably got good grades.

4. The jury was convinced that the man was innocent.
   ___ a. The man was free to go home after the trial.
   ___ b. The jury couldn't make a decision about the man's case.
   ___ c. The jury believed that the man was not at fault.
   ___ d. The jury concluded that the man was not guilty.

5. *Julie:* I just heard the news. Was anyone hurt in the fire?
   Alex: No, but the house and everything in it were destroyed.
   ___ a. The fire destroyed the house.
   ___ b. The contents of the house were destroyed in the fire.
   ___ c. The fire destroyed the contents of the house but not the house itself.
   ___ d. None of the occupants of the house was hurt in the fire.

6. The office manager's instructions for what to do with these memos were confusing to both of the secretaries.
   ___ a. The memos were confusing.
   ___ b. There are two secretaries.
   ___ c. The secretaries were confused by the instructions.
   ___ d. The secretaries' instructions were confusing to the office manager.

7. In order for us to finish cooking the whole dinner by this evening, the onions must be cut, and then the meat has to be fried. Before that, these potatoes should be washed and then peeled.

___ a. The first thing that must be done is to wash the potatoes.

___ b. Someone has to fry the onions and the meat.

___ c. The onions, meat, and potatoes have not been prepared yet.

___ d. The potatoes should be peeled after they have been washed.

8. The winners of the contest for the most successful sales records were announced by the director of the marketing department at yesterday's business meeting.

___ a. There was only one winner of the contest.

___ b. The director announced the names of the people who won the contest.

___ c. There was a business meeting yesterday.

___ d. When the director announced their names, the winners stood up at the meeting.

Exercise 7.   **TOEFL Review**

Part 1.   Completion. For items 1 through 8, circle the letter of the answer that best completes the statement or question.

1. According to the official report written by the police officers at the scene of the incident, the bank ___ at 10:00.

   a. robbed

   b. were robbed

   c. did rob

   d. was robbed

2. Bob ___ the delicious cake that was served at the company reception last week.

   a. impressed

   b. impressed with

   c. was impressed with

   d. was impressed

3. The opera ___ . It wasn't very interesting.

   a. disappointed

   b. disappointing

   c. was disappointed by

   d. was disappointing

4. The final report on this project that I have been working on ___ . Let's go out.

   a. is done

   b. is doing

   c. did

   d. are done

5. Why ___ here?

   a. was the railroad built by

   b. is the railroad to built

   c. did the railroad built

   d. was the railroad built

6. "Where were you ___ ?" If you ask Americans over the age of fifty, they can probably answer this question immediately.

   a. when President Kennedy was shot

   b. while President Kennedy was shot

   c. when President Kennedy shot

   d. while President Kennedy shot

7. ___ when the lights went out?

   a. Were you frightening

   b. Did you frighten

   c. You frightened

   d. Were you frightened

8. Your son looks too young to be in college! When ___ ?

   a. was he born

   b. did he born

   c. were he born

   d. were he borned

Part 2. Error Identification. For items 9 through 15, read each sentence carefully. Look at the underlined parts. Circle the letter that shows the incorrect part of the sentence.

9. The <u>spectators sit</u> in <u>silence</u> as the <u>amazing</u> magician continued his <u>performance</u>.
         A   B   C   D

10. The ending <u>of the</u> movie <u>was</u> so <u>surprised</u> that the audience was left <u>speechless</u>.
                A   B   C   D

11. The pilot <u>pass out</u> when the <u>air pressure</u> in <u>the</u> cockpit suddenly <u>decreased</u>, so the
               A   B   C   D

    copilot took over.

12. No one <u>in the</u> entire company <u>was</u> quite <u>sure</u> how <u>the accident was happened</u>.
             A   B   C   D

13. The <u>newly</u> office <u>furniture</u> will <u>be delivered</u> to <u>this</u> building by 5 P.M. tomorrow.
            A   B   C   D

14. When the tourists <u>were arrived</u> at <u>the</u> airport, they saw that all the flights <u>were delayed</u>
                      A   B   C

    due <u>to</u> the foul weather.
        D

15. Mayan art treasures, <u>including</u> a collection of <u>rare gold artifacts</u>, will be <u>exhibiting</u>
                           A   B   C

    next weekend <u>at the local museum downtown</u>.
                    D

Unit 8
Relative Clauses

Exercise 1. **Realia** Bumper stickers are a popular way for people to share their views on life. Look at the following bumper stickers. Write sentences describing the kind of people who put them on their car bumpers. Remember to use a relative pronoun. The first one has been done for you.

LIFE BEGINS AFTER 60

1. <u>This is a person who is over 60.</u>

2. _____

MY CHILD IS AN HONOR STUDENT at Middleton Elementary School

3. _____

Let me tell you about MY GRANDCHILDREN

4. _____

60

Rock and Roll Rules

5. _____

Honk *if you love*
SAILING!

6. _____

Exercise 2.   **Original Sentence Writing** Read the following sentences and then
write a new sentence for each by combining the two sentences.

1. The man wrote a famous novel. The novel is about life on an island in the Pacific.

   The man wrote a famous novel that is about life on an island in the Pacific.

2. The farmer had to sell his land. The farmer had a very bad harvest.

   _____

3. Lindsey just bought a new textbook. The textbook teaches molecular biology.

   _____

4. The girl is beginning to pick up a New Zealand accent. The girl's cousin is visiting her
   from New Zealand.

   _____

5. Jonathan likes to listen to music. The music has a good beat and is easy to dance to.

   _____

6. The boy had a bad automobile accident. The boy's new car is fast and expensive.

   _____

7. April likes to cook food. The food is spicy and exotic.

   _____

8. Michael wrote an angry letter to the woman. The woman is president of a computer
   company.

   _____

Exercise 3. **Realia** Look at the following work order for an apartment building. It lists all the jobs that the maintenance staff must complete by the end of the week. Use the work order to answer the questions below. Each of your answers must contain a relative clause.

Sunnyvale Arms Apartment Complex

WORK ORDER

Work for the week of: June 4–10

Tenant Name:	Tony Maruzzi
Apartment Number:	3D
Work Request:	Kitchen sink stopped up
Date Reported:	June 1
Tenant Name:	Angela Karoli
Apartment Number:	5A
Work Request:	Air conditioning doesn't work
Date Reported:	May 29
Tenant Name:	Robert Johnson
Apartment Number:	10C
Work Request:	Install new ceiling fan
Date Reported:	May 21
Tenant Name:	Julia Arriss
Apartment Number:	2A
Work Request:	Fix broken lock on sliding glass door
Date Reported:	June 2

example: Which apartment is the hottest?

The apartment that has the broken air conditioner is the hottest.

1. Which tenant has waited the longest for work to be done on his or her apartment?

_____

2. Which apartment has a stopped up kitchen sink?

_____

3. Which door needs to be fixed in apartment 2A?

_____

4. Which apartment has the most urgent problem?

_____

5. How would you describe Angela Karoli's problem?

_____

Exercise 4. **Puzzle/Game** Look at the sentences below. The underlined part of each has a mistake. Sometimes an incorrect word form has been used. Sometimes a word is missing. Write the correction or addition for each mistake in the corresponding place in the puzzle.

Across

1. The <u>computer is</u> broken won't be fixed next week.
4. When is the meeting? <u>Is</u> on Monday.
6. How many cars does he <u>owns</u>?
9. The opposite of *in* is <u>off</u>.
10. The man <u>which</u> car is in front of the bank works with my cousin.
12. Tea that has <u>iced</u> in it is called iced tea.
13. The name of the book that you <u>necessary</u> is *Mississippi at a Glance.*
16. Can you tell me if <u>her</u> and her sister are home now?
17. The name of the group <u>who</u> no one can say correctly is "Excalibur and Company."

Down

1. People <u>whom</u> live in glass houses should not throw stones. (Western proverb)
2. Wow, I can't remember ever being so <u>interesting</u> in a movie! Excellent plot!
3. <u>What</u> many people attended the business meeting?
5. All of the students finished <u>there</u> tests early.
7. Miami, <u>where</u> is the largest city in Florida, is not the capital city.
8. There is <u>not</u> good reason for this decision.
11. I've gone there only <u>one</u>, but Greg has gone there two times.

Across

18. The past forms of <u>am</u> are *was* and *were*.
19. Could you tell me the number of children that you think <u>are</u> perfect for a family?
20. <u>Have</u> you go to the store at all yesterday?
21. Only a <u>little</u> days are left until we have to return to our country.

Down

14. The teacher <u>who</u> class meets on Monday and Wednesday gives hard exams.
15. How many mistakes did you <u>do</u> on the last test? I had fourteen mistakes.
18. A <u>tricycle</u> has two wheels.
19. <u>So</u> you play very well, you can win this match. Concentrate!

Exercise 5. **Dialogue and Conversation Practice** A police officer is talking to someone who saw a bank robbery. Complete each sentence by adding a relative pronoun and using the words in the parentheses.

Police Officer: Can you tell me about the man ❶ _____

_____? (rob / bank)

Witness: When he first came in the bank, he was talking to a man

❷ _____ . (wear / red jacket)

Police Officer: Did the man in the red jacket help the robber?

Witness: No, he didn't. The robber worked by himself. The man ❸ _____

_____ (he / speak to) left before the robber

pulled out his gun.

Police Officer: What did the robber look like?

Witness: He was about 6 feet tall. He was very skinny. I could tell because he was

wearing a shirt ❹ _____ .

(be / very tight)

Police Officer: Okay. Was he carrying anything when he left?

Witness: Yes. He was carrying a black briefcase ❺ _____

_____ . (stuff / with money)

Police Officer: Thank you for your help. We will call you if we have any more questions.

Exercise 6. **Sentence Study** Read the beginning sentences. Then read the answer choices and put a check mark in front of **all of the sentences that are true** based on the beginning sentences. Remember that more than one answer is possible sometimes.

1. The man to whom Beverly is speaking is her uncle.
   ___ a. The man is Beverly's uncle.
   ___ b. Beverly is talking to one of her relatives.
   ___ c. The man is having a conversation with Beverly.
   ___ d. Beverly's uncle is talking to a man, but he is not related to Beverly.

2. Carl wants to visit a country that is very different from Canada, so Jessica told him that he should visit Nepal.
   ___ a. Carl would like to take a trip abroad.
   ___ b. Carl wants to visit a country similar to his own.
   ___ c. Jessica's point is that Nepal is very different from Canada.
   ___ d. Jessica suggested Nepal because Canada isn't a good place to visit.

3. In his search for a new house, Nathan has decided that he absolutely wants to buy a house that is large and near a river or a lake.
   ___ a. Nathan is looking for a new house.
   ___ b. Nathan's new house must be located near water.
   ___ c. Nathan's new house cannot be small.
   ___ d. Nathan does not want to live in an apartment.

4. My mother said, "No matter how hungry you might be, please do not take the cookies that are on the table in the kitchen. I made them from a special recipe that I got from Aunt Sharon, and they are for dessert tonight."
   ___ a. It's O.K. to eat the cookies now.
   ___ b. The cookies were made by Aunt Sharon.
   ___ c. It's O.K. to eat the cookies at the end of dinner.
   ___ d. The cookies are a gift for Aunt Sharon.

5. The statue that is on display in the museum's main gallery belongs to a wealthy patron.
   ___ a. The person who owns the statue is rich.
   ___ b. No one gets to see the statue because of its remote location.
   ___ c. Hardly anyone can see the statue because it is in a wealthy person's home.
   ___ d. The museum does not own the statue.

6. The students in the library are doing research for their essays.
   ___ a. The students have an assignment.
   ___ b. The students need to have information that can be found at the library.
   ___ c. The students are in the library.
   ___ d. Their essays are about the library.

7. The firefighter who rescued the little boy from the burning building received an award.
   ___ a. The little boy gave the firefighter an award.
   ___ b. A firefighter saved someone from a fire.
   ___ c. The award was given to the firefighter.
   ___ d. The little boy probably started the fire.

8. The man whose car was parked next to the fire hydrant was angry because city workers towed his car away.

___ a. The man parked his car in the wrong place.

___ b. The man's car was taken away.

___ c. The man did not park his car next to the fire hydrant.

___ d. The man was not happy about the situation.

Exercise 7.   **TOEFL Review**

Part 1.   Completion. For items 1 through 8, circle the letter of the answer that best completes the statement or question.

1. The man ___ in front of the desk is my father.

    a. who is standing

    b. whom is standing

    c. which is standing

    d. whose is standing

2. The book ___ I am reading is very interesting.

    a. whom

    b. who

    c. whose

    d. that

3. The wine ___ is from Italy.

    a. on the table that

    b. which on the table

    c. that is on the table

    d. on the table which

4. The student ___ books were stolen spoke to the police yesterday.

    a. who's

    b. whose

    c. for whom

    d. which

5. ___ I bought at the bookstore yesterday has good articles in it.

   a. The magazine that

   b. The magazine whom

   c. The magazine who

   d. The magazine whose

6. Who owns that cow ___?

   a. is in the barn

   b. that is in the barn

   c. it is in the barn

   d. that it is in the barn

7. The waiter ___ forgot my drink.

   a. whom was helping us

   b. who helping us

   c. who was helping us

   d. was helping us

8. The information ___ is not in that book.

   a. which is looking for

   b. that she looking for

   c. which she looking for

   d. that she is looking for

Part 2. Error Identification. For items 9 through 15, read each sentence carefully. Look at the underlined parts. Circle the letter that shows the incorrect part of the sentence.

9. The girl who Andrea saw her at the reception last Friday is my niece.
      A   B   C   D

10. The woman which was in the terrible car accident is in the hospital.
       A   B   C   D

11. The dog rescued a drowning boy was given an award by the mayor at a special
       A   B   C   D

ceremony last weekend.

12. Unable <u>to find</u> the <u>notes that</u> she <u>took them</u> in class yesterday, Susan <u>couldn't</u> study
             A   B   C   D

    for the exam.

13. <u>Janice put</u> the <u>beautiful flowers</u> <u>that we bought</u> her in the <u>vase is crystal</u>.
      A   B   C   D

14. <u>The rock musician</u> <u>who's music</u> I <u>admire</u> the most <u>is</u> Sting.
        A   B   C   D

15. <u>The anchorman that</u> is <u>on the local news station</u> always <u>mispronounces</u> the names of
        A   B   C

    people from <u>another</u> countries.
              D

Unit 9

Infinitives and Gerunds

Exercise 1. **Realia** Read the following advertisement for a telemarketing job. Underline the eight gerunds and infinitives in the ad.

Need a Job? Read On!

Would you like to begin a new career? Do you want to make extra money? Do you enjoy talking to new people? Have you ever considered working for a telemarketing firm? If you answered yes, then we have the answer to your needs. Come work for us at APPLEMER's.

You can practice typing (with data entry tasks). In addition, you will learn to sell our wonderful service to telephone customers.

Don't put off calling this number! There are only a few remaining openings!

We look forward to hearing from you today!

Call 1-800-123-1234

Ask for Conchita!

Exercise 2. **Original Sentence Writing** Write sentences using the words below. You may need to add some words (such as *to*) or change the form of some of the words.

1. We / expect / graduate / by next year.

   _____

2. The students / finish / take / the test / two hours ago.

   _____

3. You / want to go / swim / tomorrow afternoon?

   _____

4. Children / often / enjoy / go / to the circus.

_____

5. My parents / would like / visit / Peru.

_____

6. You / should (not) / put off / study / for next week's test.

_____

7. Carlos and Laura / postpone / get married / until next year.

_____

8. Tina / offer / give / me a ride / after class last night.

_____

Exercise 3. **Realia** Read the note that Mary has left for the baby-sitter. Write the correct form of each verb in parentheses (either a gerund or an infinitive).

Hello, Gretchen,

Here are some things that I would like you ❶ (do) _____ while I'm gone.

- I decided ❷ (make) _____ the kids go to sleep early tonight, at 8:30 p.m.

- Little Terry enjoys ❸ (watch) _____ his cartoon tape, so you can put it in the VCR for him after dinner.

- If Josephine refuses ❹ (eat) _____ her vegetables, tell her that I will bring her a surprise if she eats them all.

- If you need ❺ (contact) _____ me, the phone number here is 233-8713.

- I plan ❻ (be) _____ home by 11 p.m. at the latest.

- I know that you are not used to ❼ (use) _____ the oven, but I've already set the timer for the dinner. All you have to do is turn it on for 15 minutes.

Thanks for everything! I promise ❽ (give) _____ you more notice about baby-sitting in the future.

See you at 11!
Mary Williams

Exercise 4. **Puzzle/Game** Read the following trivia questions. Write the correct form of the verb (either a gerund or an infinitive) in each blank and then write the answer in the space provided. You may need to do some research at the library or on the Internet. If you use the Internet, you could do a search with one of the search engines. Another possibility is to use an information finder such as Ask Jeeves (or a similar service).

1. This person learned (play) _____ soccer at an early age in Brazil in the 1960s.

   _____

2. This European country avoids (get) _____ involved in wars.

   _____

3. This person put off (get) _____ married after her divorce from Sean Penn.

   _____

4. This wife of a famous political figure wanted (become) _____ the leader of the Philippines.

   _____

5. This person agreed (resign) _____ from the White House after the Watergate scandal.

   _____

6. This actor started (become) _____ popular after the movie *Titanic*.

   _____

7. People from this country enjoy (dance) _____ the samba.

   _____

8. These two countries were chosen (host) _____ the 2002 World Cup competition.

   _____

Exercise 5. **Dialogue and Conversation Practice** Roberta is telling her sister Donna about the terrible day she had. Using at least six of the verbs below, write a dialogue between Roberta and Donna.

begin	stop	need	persuade	refuse
want	promise	try	can't stand	tell

Roberta: _____

Donna: _____

Roberta: _____

Donna: _____

Roberta: _____

Donna: _____

Roberta: _____

Donna: _____

Roberta: _____

Donna: _____

Exercise 6. **Sentence Study** Read the beginning sentences. Then read the answer choices and put a check mark in front of **all of the sentences that are true** based on the beginning sentences. Remember that more than one answer is possible sometimes.

1. On his way home from work, Billy stopped to pick up his laundry. It was his only stop.
   ___ a. Billy didn't pick up his laundry.
   ___ b. Billy picked up his laundry when he was going home.
   ___ c. Billy left work, picked up his laundry, and then went home.
   ___ d. Billy picked up his laundry, and then he went to work.

2. Gretchen agreed to accept our invitation to go to the concert with us.
   ___ a. Gretchen asked us to go with her to the concert.
   ___ b. Gretchen decided to attend the concert with us.
   ___ c. Gretchen didn't come with us to the concert.
   ___ d. Gretchen wanted to see the concert, but she could not go with us.

3. Julie's dad cooks spaghetti three or four times a week, and she is really tired of eating spaghetti.
    ___ a. Julie needs to rest more.
    ___ b. Julie's dad cooks the same dish a lot.
    ___ c. Julie would prefer to eat something different.
    ___ d. Julie's favorite food is spaghetti.

4. Tracy promised to give me her dictionary.
    ___ a. Tracy promised to give me her dictionary.
    ___ b. I promised Tracy a dictionary.
    ___ c. I promised to give Tracy her dictionary.
    ___ d. Tracy needs a dictionary now.

5. Luisa and Tony are planning a trip, but they are still not sure of their ultimate destination. However, they know that they'd like to travel around the end of next month.
    ___ a. Someone is planning a trip for them.
    ___ b. They are not going on a trip next month, but they would like to take a vacation.
    ___ c. They are planning to go on a trip, but they do not know when.
    ___ d. They are planning to go on a trip, but they do not know where.

6. According to Annabelle's friends, there are several reasons that she has decided to call off the wedding.
    ___ a. The bride called up her friends to tell them about the wedding.
    ___ b. She postponed her friend's wedding.
    ___ c. The exact reasons for her decision are not given in this sentence.
    ___ d. The wedding will not happen.

7. After three attempts to call my family in Romania, I finally tried calling the operator, who was able to put my call through on the first try.
    ___ a. I couldn't reach the operator.
    ___ b. I tried the operator four times.
    ___ c. I used the operator to help me make my call.
    ___ d. My family in Romania tried to call me several times.

8. People usually don't remember sleepwalking and often say that they have never done it.
    ___ a. These people do not sleepwalk.
    ___ b. These people do not remember that they have sleepwalked.
    ___ c. These people sleepwalk, but it makes them remember to sleep.
    ___ d. These people have a difficult time trying to sleep after they have sleepwalked.

Exercise 7. **TOEFL Review**

Part 1. Completion. For items 1 through 8, circle the letter of the item that best completes the statement or question.

1. Larry told us ___ .

   a. wait for him at his home

   b. waiting for him at his home

   c. to waiting for him at his home

   d. to wait for him at his home

2. The manager didn't allow ___ .

   a. have a company party for his employees

   b. his employees to have a company party

   c. his employees having a company party

   d. company party for his employees

3. ___ can be a wonderful experience.

   a. Fly a hot air balloon

   b. To flying a hot air balloon

   c. Flown a hot air balloon

   d. Flying a hot air balloon

4. My little brother ___ .

   a. can't to stand to watch horror movies

   b. can't stand watching horror movies

   c. can't stand to watching horror movies

   d. watching horror movies can't stand

5. Do you want ___ ?

   a. that we go to dinner later on this evening

   b. going to dinner later on this evening

   c. to go to dinner later on this evening

   d. go to dinner later on this evening

6. Did you write down what the teacher __ ?

   a. told us to study

   b. said us to study

   c. told us study

   d. said us studying

7. __ because her doctor warned her of the consequences.

   a. Sally stopped to smoke

   b. Sally stopped to smoking

   c. Sally smoked not

   d. Sally stopped smoking

8. Would you and Sherman like __ ?

   a. going on vacation to Europe next year

   b. go on vacation to Europe next year

   c. to going on vacation to Europe next year

   d. to go on vacation to Europe next year

Part 2. Error Identification. For items 9 through 15, read each sentence carefully. Look at the underlined parts. Circle the letter that shows the incorrect part of the sentence.

9. The kids <u>refused doing</u> their homework because <u>they</u> wanted <u>to watch</u> a special <u>program</u>.
           A   B   C   D

10. I want <u>to eat</u> in <u>the</u> restaurant <u>who</u> opened last month at the <u>new commercial center</u>.
           A   B   C   D

11. Mary and Herbert made me <u>to drive</u> them home <u>after</u> the play because <u>their</u> car had
                               A   B   C

    <u>a problem</u>.
      D

12. Can <u>you</u> have your boss <u>call</u> me after he's <u>finished to attend</u> his <u>meeting</u>?
         A   B   C   D

13. According to most <u>pediatricians</u>, babies <u>usually</u> stop <u>crying</u> after their first teeth
                     A   B   C

    <u>comes</u> in.
     D

14. <u>To understanding</u> regional accents <u>takes</u> a lot <u>of</u> practice and <u>patience</u>.
       A   B   C   D

15. <u>My guidance counselor</u> advised <u>to me</u> to <u>register</u> for two <u>other</u> classes as well.
        A   B   C   D

Unit 10

Connectors

Exercise 1.   **Realia** Ahmad wants to attend Lantic University. Read the essay that he has written as part of his application. Correct any errors that you find. You may also want to combine some sentences and/or omit some punctuation to improve the essay.

Application: Lantic University

As part of the application process, please write an essay explaining why you want to attend this school. Include any strengths and weaknesses that you have.

    I want to attended the Lantic University so that I can earn a degree in civil engineering. I have be studying advanced math for several years, therefore, I think that I do very well in your program. One of my weaknesses is reading; but, I have strong time management skills, and I alway allow plenty of time to complete the read assignments. My father is an engineer, and I want to become one, to, so that I can work at his company when I graduate.

Exercise 2.   **Original Sentence Writing** Read the following sentences. For each, using the words given, write a sentence or question using a connector in parentheses.

1. Why did you go to Rome? (in order to)

    _____

2. Why do you want to study English? (because)

    _____

3. Rosa wants to see Eric Clapton. (Jose / too)

_____

4. Gary was in Idaho last year. (Henry / too)

_____

5. Sandra doesn't know how to speak English. (Linda / either)

_____

6. Mary swims every day. (Joe / not)

_____

7. Nancy drives to school. (Oscar / however / walk)

_____

8. I brought three pencils. (so / would have / enough)

_____

_____

Exercise 3.   **Realia** Our school has performed a study that compares two private high schools, Easton High and Lincoln Academy. Below is a summary of our results. Write a paragraph using the table explaining the differences and similarities. Use the connectors you have learned in this chapter.

	Easton High	Lincoln Academy
Tuition	$2,535/semester	$4,500/semester
Enrollment	200 students/semester	150 students/semester
Number of countries represented	25	28
Number of hours studied per week	25	25
Percentage of students who go to a university when they finish	75%	15%

_____

_____

_____

_____

_____

_____

_____

_____

_____

Exercise 4. **Puzzle/Game** Read the clues for the crossword puzzle. Then fill in the answers in the puzzle.

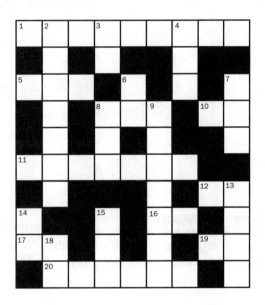

Across

1. Marcus is from Switzerland. _____ , he might speak French, German, or Italian—or even all three.

5. Jill bought a new book, and Randy did too. How many new books did these two people buy?

Down

2. February has 28 days. _____ , every four years it has 29 days. This is called leap year.

3. This is a prefix that means "to do again."

4. The airplane took _____ at exactly noon.

Across

8. My father has brown eyes, _____ my mother does, too.

10. He went to the post office _____ mail an important letter.

11. September doesn't have 31 days, and _____ does April.

12. _____ it rains, then the coach might call off the game.

16. It rained really hard all day, _____ the coach decided to call off the game.

17. You can have cake _____ pie but not both.

19. The man asked the little boy, "What do you want to _____ when you grow up?"

20. September doesn't have 31 days, and April doesn't, _____ .

Down

6. She was born _____ October.

7. I went to the post office _____ some stamps.

8. It's a kind of museum or a kind of class in school.

9. Ashley doesn't play tennis very well, _____ _____ ? (2 words)

13. This means that you don't have to pay any money for something.

14. I wrote the note _____ be able to remember the things that I had to buy at the store.

15. Monday was a very bad day, _____ Tuesday was a great day!

18. It's the same as number 3 down.

Exercise 5. **Dialogue and Conversation Practice** Caroline and Betty have just met. They are getting to know each other. Write a dialogue using connectors. Use the vocabulary words below.

mother	brothers	job	either	but . . . don't
however	therefore	too	so	and . . . too

Caroline: _____

Betty: _____

Caroline: _____

Betty: _____

Caroline: _____

Betty: _____

Caroline: _____

Betty: _____

Caroline: _____

Betty: _____

Caroline: _____

Betty: _____

Exercise 6.　　**Sentence Study**　Read the beginning sentences. Then read the answer choices and put a check mark in front of **all of the sentences that are true** based on the beginning sentences. Remember that more than one answer is possible sometimes.

1. John knows how to make chocolate, and Larry does too.
   ___ a. Only John knows how to make chocolate.
   ___ b. Only Larry knows how to make chocolate.
   ___ c. They both know how to make chocolate.
   ___ d. Larry knows how to make chocolate, and so does John.

2. We were surprised to find out that Yoko speaks Chinese, but Rita doesn't.
   ___ a. Rita and Yoko speak Chinese.
   ___ b. Yoko speaks Chinese.
   ___ c. Rita speaks Chinese.
   ___ d. Yoko and Rita don't speak Chinese.

3. I didn't finish the test, but Joe did.
   ___ a. I answered only some of the questions.
   ___ b. Joe answered only some of the questions.
   ___ c. I answered more questions than Joe did.
   ___ d. Unlike me, Joe answered all of the questions.

4. Palmer likes to swim and he is good at it; however, he is too young to swim alone.
   ___ a. Palmer can swim alone because he likes to swim.
   ___ b. Palmer is a good swimmer, so he swims alone.
   ___ c. Palmer can't swim alone because he is too young.
   ___ d. Palmer is a good swimmer.

5. My husband is Armenian, but I am American. However, we live in the United States.
   ___ a. We are both American.
   ___ b. We are both Armenian.
   ___ c. Only my husband is American.
   ___ d. Only I am American.

6. Sometimes Hal and Jill play Monopoly against Carry and Lisa. Hal and Jill really don't like to play Monopoly because they're not so good at it, but Carry and Lisa are crazy about this game.
   ___ a. Carry and Lisa probably play Monopoly more than Hal and Jill do.
   ___ b. When these four play Monopoly, Carry and Lisa probably win.
   ___ c. Hal and Jill play Monopoly, and they are very good at it.
   ___ d. Carry and Lisa enjoy playing Monopoly.

7. Jimmy has three daughters, and so does his brother Richard. This means that Jimmy has three nieces, and Richard does, too.
   ___ a. Jimmy has only two children.
   ___ b. Richard has three daughters and no sons.
   ___ c. Only Richard has three daughters.
   ___ d. Jimmy and Richard are related.

8. Katrina is a good basketball player, so no one is surprised when she scores a lot of points in a game.
   ___ a. Katrina's teammates probably do not want her to shoot the ball.
   ___ b. The spectators find it difficult to believe that Katrina scores a lot of points.
   ___ c. When Katrina scores a lot of points in a game, people are not surprised.
   ___ d. The fact that Katrina scores a lot of points in a game is not surprising.

Exercise 7.   **TOEFL Review**

Part 1.   Completion. For items 1 through 8, circle the letter of the answer that best completes the statement.

1. Larry is a basketball player, ___ .

   a. but Joe doesn't

   b. and so does Joe

   c. but Joe isn't

   d. and Joe does too

2. He learned to sing ___ .

   a. in order to play the part in the movie

   b. so play the part in the movie

   c. at the girl

   d. for play the part in the movie

3. My mother walks every day, ___ .

    a. and so my father does

    b. and my father is too

    c. and so does my father

    d. and so is my father

4. Carol doesn't like spaghetti, ___ .

    a. and Ed doesn't either

    b. and neither is Ed

    c. and Ed isn't either

    d. and neither Ed does

5. You should study tonight, ___ .

    a. and Tina should

    b. and so Tina should

    c. and so should Tina

    d. and Tina shouldn't

6. I didn't like the movie, ___ .

    a. and Sara did

    b. but Sara did

    c. so Sara did

    d. but Sara didn't

7. Melanie can see well; ___ needs to wear glasses.

    a. however, she

    b. but she

    c. and she

    d. so she

8. Jamie bought a house; ___ .

    a. therefore, he had to buy new furniture

    b. however, he bought furniture, too

    c. but he didn't bought furniture

    d. and he buys furniture

Part 2. Error Identification. For items 9 through 15, read each sentence carefully. Look at the underlined parts. Circle the letter that shows the incorrect part of the sentence.

9. Jane is <u>an avid</u> football fan; <u>however</u>, she <u>doesn't go</u> to every <u>games</u>.
          A   B   C   D

10. James <u>knows how</u> to drive, <u>but</u> Billy <u>haven't</u> learned <u>yet</u>.
            A   B   C   D

11. The top player on the Brazilian <u>team do not have</u> good <u>running</u> skills; <u>however</u>, the
                          A   B   C

    top player on <u>the Italian team does</u>.
              D

12. Mr. Williams, <u>who used to be</u> an international copyright lawyer, owns the flower shop
               A

    <u>in the center of town</u>, but he <u>is thinking</u> about <u>sell</u> it in the near future.
         B   C   D

13. Chemistry and physics are <u>two of the most</u> demanding courses <u>for</u> most new students,
                     A   B

    but <u>courses such as art and</u> music <u>are rarely</u>.
          C   D

14. <u>Without extra financial help</u> in the form of <u>govern</u> aid <u>funded</u> by taxes, it is doubtful
          A   B   C

    that many of the social services <u>that we hold</u> so dear could be provided.
                            D

15. Camels, commonly found in <u>certain areas of Asia</u> as well <u>as</u> areas of the Middle East,
                       A   B

    <u>are known to spit</u> when <u>they becomes angry</u> or feel threatened.
         C   D

Unit 11

VERB + Direct
or Indirect Object

Exercise 1. **Realia** Ms. Jones is an ESL teacher. Today she is teaching her class some pronunciation. Read the following transcript from Ms. Jones's class. Underline the six phrases that have the following pattern: VERB + object + *to/for.*

> Class, today I'm going to introduce a new sound to you. It's called the *schwa* sound, and it is very commonly used in English.
>
> Let me explain the pronunciation to you. This sound, often represented with the letters *uh*, is similar to the sound many people make when they don't know what to say. The *schwa* sound can also be achieved when you get the wind knocked out of you, as if a soccer ball hits your stomach.
>
> Now, please open your mouths for me, just a little bit. Take your fist and hit your stomach lightly, not too hard.
>
> Very good. Here are some common words with the schwa sound. I will pronounce the words for you. Then you can repeat the words to me after I say them.
>
> If you want me to answer a question for you, please raise your hand.

Exercise 2. **Original Sentence Writing** Read the following words and write sentences using the words given below. You may have to change the order of some of the phrases. Add articles where necessary.

1. I / gave / book / Lisa.

_____

2. The teacher / (neg) explained / lesson / me.

_____

3. The bank teller / cashed / check / my mother.

_____

4. My manager / introduced / me / his wife.

_____

5. Can you describe / your country / me?

_____

6. The police officer / asked / some questions/ us.

_____

7. The plane ticket / cost / 500 dollars / him.

_____

8. Thelma / offered / a ride home / after class / me.

_____

_____

Exercise 3. **Realia** Michelle had a wonderful birthday, and she wrote about it in her diary. Read Michelle's diary entry. Circle each of the correct objects in parentheses.

April 12, 2000

Dear Diary,

What a great day today was! It was my birthday, and my parents gave

❶ (me, to me) a wonderful gift... a new stereo system! I told ❷ (to

them, them) that I wanted one, but I never thought they would give one

❸ (to me, for me). It was wonderful! I'm sure it cost ❹ (to them,

them) a lot of money. I asked ❺ (them, for them) if they had a hard

time finding it, but they said my brother Joey helped ❻ (them, for them)

choose it. Joey suggested this new model ❼ (to Dad and Mom, Dad

and Mom), and they agreed! It's unbelievable! Then all my friends came

over and wished ❽ (to me, me) a happy birthday. What a day! I'll write

you again tomorrow!

Exercise 4. **Puzzle/Game** Read the following questions and then write the correct answers in the space provided. You may need to do some research at the library or on the Internet. If you use the Internet, you could do a search with one of the search engines such as Excite or Yahoo. Another possibility is to use an information finder service such as Ask Jeeves (or a similar service).

1. In what country can you use the currency *lire* to buy things? _____
2. In what U.S. state can you buy your friend a Seminole tribe souvenir? _____
3. In what year did people see France win the World Cup? _____
4. In what city can tourists visit the Great Pyramids? _____
5. In what century did people begin to appreciate Pablo Picasso's paintings? _____
6. In what country can you take a lorry to Buckingham Palace? _____
7. In what language can you read a book from right to left? _____
8. In what U.S. state can tourists find a souvenir of a NASA space shuttle? _____

Exercise 5. **Dialogue and Conversation Practice** Bobby and Susan are having an argument about what to buy their mother for her birthday. Write a dialogue using all the verbs below. Remember to use the correct VERB + direct or indirect object construction. Underline the VERB + direct/indirect object constructions in your dialogue.

show	buy	find	get	make	cost

Bobby: _____

Susan: _____

Bobby: _____

Susan: _____

Bobby: _____

Susan: _____

Bobby: _____

Susan: _____

Bobby: _____

Susan: _____

Exercise 6. | **Sentence Study** Read the beginning sentences. Then read the answer choices and put a check mark in front of **all of the sentences that are true** based on the beginning sentences. Remember that more than one answer is possible sometimes.

1. Debbie made me dinner tonight.
   ___ a. She cooked for me.
   ___ b. She cooked dinner, and I ate it.
   ___ c. We went to a restaurant.
   ___ d. I usually cook dinner, but Debbie cooked dinner tonight.

2. I really wanted to go on the trip to France. The price of the plane ticket was $800, but unfortunately I could only afford half of that amount.
   ___ a. I paid $800 for the ticket.
   ___ b. I needed an additional $400.
   ___ c. I didn't buy the $800 ticket.
   ___ d. The ticket was too expensive for me.

3. When I bought my new TV, I paid $120. I was able to get this cheap price because I had a discount coupon that saved me $40.
   ___ a. The price that I paid was $120.
   ___ b. The original price of the TV was $160.
   ___ c. I saved $40.
   ___ d. The TV that I purchased was new.

4. The child asked his mother a question.
   ___ a. The mother wanted to know something.
   ___ b. The child wanted to know something.
   ___ c. They both had a question.
   ___ d. Neither of them had a question.

5. I gave my cat a treat, and she ate it immediately.
   ___ a. My cat gave me a treat.
   ___ b. My cat received a treat.
   ___ c. The person that I gave my cat to gave it a treat.
   ___ d. My cat received something good to eat.

6. The announcer repeated the final score to the audience, but some people still could not believe that the Miami team won.
   ___ a. The Miami team won, but no one could believe it.
   ___ b. No one could believe that the Miami team was the winner.
   ___ c. The announcer said the score at least two times.
   ___ d. Some people did not believe that the announcer said the score twice.

7. I couldn't believe it. I thought I was going to receive a refund, but my credit card company charged me extra last month.
___ a. I had to pay extra money.
___ b. I was surprised.
___ c. My credit card company called me up.
___ d. My credit card company gave me a refund.

8. Although it was not really her responsibility, Janet reluctantly found it necessary to do the work for John because it was beyond his ability.
___ a. John could not do the work.
___ b. John did all the work, and Janet did, too.
___ c. Janet was eager to help John with the work.
___ d. Janet did the work for John.

Exercise 7.   **TOEFL Review**

Part 1.   Completion. For items 1 through 8, circle the letter of the item that best completes the statement or question.

1. Can you please pass ___ ?

   a. me the newspaper

   b. the newspaper for me

   c. the newspaper me

   d. to me the newspaper

2. Larry described ___ .

   a. to us his vacation

   b. his vacation to us

   c. his vacation for us

   d. us his vacation

3. We mentioned ___ .

   a. the plan to our supervisor

   b. our supervisor the plan

   c. to our supervisor the plan

   d. the plan for our supervisor

4. Maria's classmates wished ___ .

    a. for her a happy birthday

    b. to her a happy birthday

    c. a happy birthday for her

    d. her a happy birthday

5. I lent ___ .

    a. to Tony my electronic dictionary

    b. my electronic dictionary for Tony

    c. Tony my electronic dictionary

    d. for Tony my electronic dictionary

6. Did you buy ___ ?

    a. a present to your husband

    b. a present for your husband

    c. to your husband a present

    d. for your husband a present

7. The main cook in the home of a wealthy family had many duties, including

    making ___ .

    a. dinner the children

    b. dinner to the children

    c. dinner for the children

    d. the children for dinner

8. ___ the contract to her administrative assistant.

    a. Ms. Lincoln brought

    b. Ms. Lincoln made

    c. Ms. Lincoln found

    d. Ms. Lincoln asked

Part 2.   Error Identification. For items 9 through 15, read each sentence carefully. Look at the underlined parts. Circle the letter that shows the incorrect part of the sentence.

9. A kind young man opened the door to me yesterday while I was shopping at the mall.
    A   B   C   D

10. The dermatologist prescribe some very potent and expensive medication for me
    A   B   C

    because of my skin problem.
    D

11. If you ask her nicely, I'm sure she will be able to do a favor you.
         A   B   C   D

12. Although most courses have a final exam during the last class meeting, some
                A

    professors opt to give a take-home final, which is an exam that students receive
               B   C

    ahead of time, completed it at home, and then bring to the last class meeting.
                    D

13. Gilda was the hit of the party; she was introduced for everyone, and they liked her!
          A   B   C   D

14. In order to improve my reading, my counselor suggested an interesting books to me.
              A   B   C   D

15. Because I didn't understand the lecture, I talked to my professor after class and
                A   B

    asked him to repeat me the information.
          C   D

Unit 12

Review

Exercise 1. **Realia** Chocolate: fact or fiction? Look at the groups of words below. Rearrange the words in each group so that they make a grammatically correct sentence. If the sentence is true, write T on the line. If the sentence is false, write F. You may need to do some research at the library or on the Internet. If you use the Internet, you could do a search with one of the search engines such as Yahoo or Excite. Another possibility is to use an information finder service such as Ask Jeeves (or a similar service).

___ 1. to cause cavities has not been proven or tooth decay Chocolate.

_____

_____

___ 2. he found a Spanish ship was visiting what is now Honduras, When Christopher Columbus with cocoa beans in it.

_____

_____

___ 3. is white on the inside and The fruit of the cocoa tree green on the outside.

_____

_____

___ 4. consists of saturated fat, which can cause heart disease Chocolate.

_____

_____

___ 5. they would have to put a health warning label on their products were worried about recent research Chocolate companies because they thought.

_____

_____

Exercise 2. ▐Original Sentence Writing▌ In this book, you have practiced several verb tenses. You have learned some new verb tenses and reviewed some that you studied in Books 1 and 2. In this exercise, write a statement or question with the words given below. The verb should be in the verb tense that is indicated.

1. you / take out / the garbage? (past)

   _____

   _____

2. I / watch / TV / when / pizza / come (past progressive)

   _____

   _____

3. Julia / never / travel / to Japan (present perfect)

   _____

   _____

4. you / must / drive / careful / so / you / not / get into / accident (present)

   _____

   _____

5. tree / decorate / children (past tense, passive voice)

   _____

   _____

6. that / be (present) / boy / I / meet (past) / last year

   _____

   _____

7. I / like / read / books / in order to / learn / about different countries (present)

   _____

   _____

8. My parents / buy / me / new car (past)

   _____

   _____

Exercise 3. **Realia** Find an interesting photograph or drawing from a magazine or a newspaper. Paste or attach it here. Write one paragraph about what you see in the picture. Make sure you include the following grammar points:

1. passive voice
2. relative clauses
3. gerunds
4. infinitives
5. connectors
6. verbs with direct or indirect objects

Underline each example of these grammar points in your paragraph and put the corresponding number (1, 2, 3, etc.) above your examples.

_____

_____

_____

_____

_____

_____

_____

_____

_____

_____

_____

_____

_____

_____

_____

_____

_____

Exercise 4. **Puzzle/Game** Read the clues for the crossword puzzle. Then fill in the answers in the puzzle.

Across

1. The book _____ he is reading is excellent.

4. We went there _____ car.

5. _____ you ever flown on the Concorde?

7. Are you interested _____ going to the beach with us?

8. I was surprised _____ the color of her dress.

9. The past participle of this verb is the same as its past tense form.

11. When you are _____ with the stapler, may I use it?

13. It's the liquid in a pen.

14. It's important to try _____ shoes before you buy them.

17. It's a short greeting.

19. He insisted _____ going to the park by bike.

20. While the first customs official was _____ our suitcases, the other customs official was looking at our passports.

21. What terrible food! I'm _____ by the smell of it.

Down

2. The teacher said, "Time is up. Please _____ _____ your papers now." (2 words)

3. I'd like to _____ you for helping today.

4. The past participle of this verb is the same as its present tense form, but its past tense form is different.

6. I didn't eat any sweets yesterday or the day before, but I _____ some cake last week.

10. Do you think that _____ a shower or a bath uses more water?

12. If it's cold outside, you should put _____ a sweater before leaving the house.

14. In my life, I've _____ a total of six cars.

15. Amsterdam is located in _____ Netherlands.

16. How many days _____ a leap year have?

18. The player was disappointed _____ his results.

19. I've gone to Africa only _____ . That trip was in 2000.

Exercise 5. **Dialogue and Conversation Practice** Ahmed, Joanna, and Krikor
are on vacation in Washington, D.C. They are planning their
activities for the rest of the week. Write a dialogue using as many of
the grammar points covered in this book as possible. The
vocabulary below will get you started.

Smithsonian	Washington Monument	White House	visit
Lincoln Memorial	build	the president	cherry trees
see	tour	Vietnam Memorial	

_____

_____

_____

_____

_____

_____

_____

_____

_____

_____

_____

_____

OUR NATION REMEMBERS
THE COURAGE, SACRIFICE,
AND DEVOTION TO DUTY
AND COUNTRY OF ITS
VIETNAM VETERANS

Exercise 6. **Sentence Study** Read the beginning sentences. Then read the answer choices and put a check mark in front of **all of the sentences that are true** based on the beginning sentences. Remember that more than one answer is possible sometimes.

1. The book he is reading is scary.
   ___ a. He finished it already.
   ___ b. He is not finished yet.
   ___ c. He is still reading the book.
   ___ d. The book is frightening.

2. Ann was sleeping when Barbara came home.
   ___ a. First, Ann went to sleep. Then Barbara came home.
   ___ b. First, Barbara came home. Then Ann went to sleep.
   ___ c. Ann went to sleep. At the same time, Barbara came home.
   ___ d. Barbara came home after Ann woke up.

3. I am used to eating at a restaurant once a week.
   ___ a. I don't do that anymore.
   ___ b. It's a habit. I go every week.
   ___ c. I go twice a week.
   ___ d. I do this, but I do not really like to do it.

4. The instructor for the class said, "Your paper must be done by Wednesday. No late papers will be accepted."
   ___ a. The students must finish their paper by Wednesday.
   ___ b. The instructor announced the deadline for submitting the paper.
   ___ c. Students may receive extra time to work on the paper.
   ___ d. It is not acceptable to turn in the paper on Thursday.

5. That book that I read last month was written by Laura Ingalls Wilder.
   ___ a. Laura Ingalls Wilder wrote the book.
   ___ b. The book was published last month.
   ___ c. I read this book last month.
   ___ d. This is not the first book that I have read by this author.

6. He went to the game so he could see his favorite team play.
   ___ a. He saw his favorite team play.
   ___ b. He didn't go to the game.
   ___ c. He didn't see his favorite team play.
   ___ d. He is going to the game tomorrow.

7. The cake was not a success because the correct number of eggs was not added at the correct time.

   ___ a. The cake required eggs.

   ___ b. The cake tasted good.

   ___ c. The cook did not add the right number of eggs.

   ___ d. The cake needed more sugar in order to taste better.

8. While the students were taking the final exam for their history course, the instructor stood in the front of the room to make sure that no one tried to copy another student's answers.

   ___ a. The teacher left the room during the test.

   ___ b. The teacher wanted to make sure that no one cheated on the test.

   ___ c. The test was a final exam.

   ___ d. The teacher was in the front of the classroom.

Exercise 7.   **TOEFL Review**

Part 1.   Completion. For items 1 through 8, circle the letter of the answer that best completes the statement.

1. I need someone to _____ the cats while I'm gone. They need to be fed twice a day.

   a. watch out for

   b. look for

   c. look after

   d. look into

2. I _____ on the computer.

   a. study while you working

   b. studied while you work

   c. studying while you worked

   d. was studying while you were working

3. Lucille _____ her mother only three times since 1998.

   a. visiting

   b. was visiting

   c. visited

   d. has visited

4. She delivered the package _____ .

   a. on hand

   b. by hand

   c. with her hands

   d. in hand

5. If you do not understand the assignment, you need to speak _____ your teacher.

   a. on

   b. through

   c. at

   d. to

6. The stadium _____ in 1997 after the local tax increase was approved.

   a. be built

   b. did build

   c. was built

   d. were built

7. Everyone agrees that the sofa _____ .

   a. that bought is beautiful

   b. you bought are beautiful

   c. that you buy is beautiful

   d. you bought is beautiful

8. _____ Mount Everest is extremely difficult, even for those with sophisticated equipment and rigorous physical training.

   a. To climbing

   b. Climbing

   c. Climb

   d. Climbed

Part 2. Error Identification. For items 9 through 15, read each sentence carefully. Look at the underlined parts. Circle the letter that shows the incorrect part of the sentence.

9. Jason mowed <u>the</u> lawn early <u>in the</u> morning <u>so he could</u> watch <u>football game</u> that
           A   B   C   D

afternoon.

10. I will <u>pick up you</u> at 10:00 <u>after</u> I finish <u>studying</u> for <u>my math exam</u>.
           A   B   C   D

11. The ambassador to Senegal <u>is depart</u> Toronto tomorrow <u>on the evening flight</u> to New
                            A   B

York, <u>but</u> several <u>of her assistants</u> will remain.
     C   D

12. The CD <u>that</u> I <u>like</u> the <u>better</u> is Ottmar Liebert's *Nouveau Flamenco,* but there are
          A   B   C

many that I find very <u>good</u>.
                D

13. With vacation <u>coming</u> soon, the children are <u>understandably excited</u> about going <u>in</u>
              A   B   C

Hawaii <u>next</u> month.
     D

14. The <u>announcement made</u> by the chairperson <u>was hear</u> by everyone <u>who was</u> in the
          A   B   C

building <u>at that time</u>.
       D

15. <u>Have you ever be</u> to California before? Many people say <u>that</u> it's <u>one of the most</u>
    A   B   C

beautiful states <u>in the</u> United States!
         D

Answer Key

Unit 1

Ex. 1, p. 1: the → an, becomed → became, Helens → Helen's, she → her, wilder → wilder than, had → was, too → very, teached → taught, did entered → entered, Annes' → Anne's

Ex. 2, p. 2: Answers will vary.

Ex. 3, p. 2: 1. Angela spent $41.30 on March 7. 2. The most expensive thing (that) she bought was fish. 3. The soup costs the same as the bread. 4. The dog food was more expensive than the fish. 5. March 14 was cheaper for Angela. 6. Angela spent $67.71 for both trips to the store. 7. A gallon of milk costs $3.75. 8. Angela bought a tomato both times.

Ex. 4, p. 4:

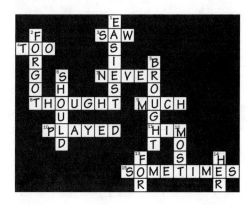

Ex. 5, p. 5: 1. ∅ 2. do you want 3. the 4. the 5. very 6. hottest 7. cooler 8. should 9. coldest 10. very 11. will 12. always 13. never 14. one 15. didn't know 16. ∅

Ex. 6, p. 6: 1. abc 2. bc 3. bc 4. a 5. bd 6. bc 7. a 8. ad

Ex. 7, p. 7: 1. d 2. c 3. b 4. c 5. d 6. d 7. a 8. b 9. A 10. B 11. D 12. A 13. A 14. A 15. B

Unit 2

Ex. 1, p. 10: called him up, find out, turned it off, put on, figure it out, took off, took out

Ex. 2, p. 10: Answers will vary. Suggested answers: 1. I need to clean it up. 2. I need to put it out. 3. I should put it away. 4. I should turn the music down. 5. I should look it up. 6. I'm going to pick it up. 7. I need to look it up. 8. I have to call the party off.

Ex. 3, p. 11: 1. up 2. out 3. away 4. out (OR/away) 5. back 6. on 7. up (OR back) 8. out

Ex. 4, p. 12: get through, get over, get along with, found out 1. Alaska 2. winter 3. water 4. heart 5. After locking the door and all the windows, she stabbed herself with an icicle she got from outside. The icicle melted from the heat in the room. That is why there was a pool of water under the body and no evidence of a weapon.

Ex. 5, p. 13: Answers will vary.

Ex. 6, p. 13: 1. cd 2. ac 3. ad 4. ad 5. d 6. bd 7. acd 8. bcd

Ex. 7, p. 14: 1. b 2. c 3. d 4. c 5. c 6. d 7. a 8. d 9. D 10. C 11. B 12. C 13. B 14. D 15. D

Unit 3

Ex. 1, p. 17: 1. Sarah was reading (her) mail at 9 A.M. 2. Ryan was calling clients at 9 A.M. 3. Sarah was meeting with Mr. Green while Ryan was reading (his) mail. 4. Sarah was eating lunch while she was typing her report. 5. They were meeting with their supervisor at 1 P.M. 6. Ryan was writing memos while he was returning phone calls. 7. Ryan was finishing his financial report at 4 P.M. 8. Ryan was picking up the dog from the vet while Sarah was at the gym.

Ex. 2, p. 18: Answers will vary.

Ex. 3, p. 19: 1. Mr. Applewhite was driving south on Broad Avenue. 2. When he stopped his car, the car behind him hit him. 3. Mr. Applewhite got out of his car when the other driver hit him. 4. The other driver was talking to his passenger while Mr. Appplewhite was calling the police. 5. When the police arrived, they gave the other driver a ticket (for reckless driving).

Ex. 4, p. 20: 1. breaking 2. laughing 3. urging 4. humming 5. dancing 6. running 7. padding 8. losing 9. entering 10. sewing The answer: A human does.

Ex. 5, p. 20: 1. was standing 2. walked 3. did you do 4. saw 5. did he say 6. did 7. were talking 8. stared / was staring 9. signed 10. were ringing

Ex. 6, p. 22: 1. c 2. d 3. bd 4. c 5. abc 6. c 7. ac 8. abcd

Ex. 7, p. 23: 1. b 2. a 3. c 4. d 5. c 6. a 7. b 8. a 9. D 10. A 11. B 12. B 13. B 14. C 15. B

Unit 4

Ex. 1, p. 26: Answers will vary.

Ex. 2, p. 26: (Each answer has two sentences. The second sentence of each answer will vary.) 1. Jack *has gone* to that theater many times. 2. *Have* you *driven* to Miami before? 3. Mr. and Mrs. Volks *haven't lived* here very long. 4. *Have* you *fed* the cats yet? 5. No, I *have been* in a meeting for the last three hours. 6. I *have been taking* knitting lessons for the last three months. 7. *Haven't* you *watered* those plants yet? 8. *Have* you ever *gone* to California?

Ex. 3, p. 28: 1. the most interesting city I have (OR I've) ever visited. 2. haven't (OR have not) been to Broadway yet 3. I've (OR I have) been to a lot of restaurants 4. Have you ever been to the Metropolitan Museum? 5. I've (OR I have) gone there

Ex. 4, p. 28:

Ex. 5, p. 29: Answers will vary.

Ex. 6, p. 30: 1. cd 2. c 3. bcd 4. abcd 5. ac 6. bcd 7. bc 8. d

Ex. 7, p. 31: 1. c 2. a 3. c 4. b 5. d 6. b 7. b 8. c 9. C 10. B 11. A 12. B 13. B 14. B 15. D

Unit 5

Ex. 1, p. 34: 1. hard 2. well 3. really 4. quickly 5. easily 6. automatically 7. clearly 8. fluently 9. wholeheartedly

Ex. 2, p. 35: (Each answer has two sentences. The second sentence of each answer will vary.) 1. Barbara takes notes quickly. 2. The teacher told us to arrive to class punctually. 3. Lucia answered the test questions easily. 4. Bobby happily left school. 5. The schoolchildren cross the street carefully. 6. Maryanne silently received the doctor's evaluation. 7. Louise boxes excellently. 8. The painters repainted our home poorly OR badly.

Ex. 3, p. 36: 1. by 2. by writing 3. By not 4. By 5. with 6. by 7. by 8. by

Ex. 4, p. 36: 1. speaking 2. exercising 3. joining 4. doing 5. brushing 6. taking 7. watching
Answer: By ironing them.

Ex. 5, p. 37: Answers will vary.

Ex. 6, p. 38: 1. c 2. ad 3. bd 4. abc 5. bd 6. cd 7. abcd 8. ac

Ex. 7, p. 40: 1. b 2. b 3. b 4. c 5. d 6. b 7. b 8. c 9. A 10. B 11. D 12. B 13. D 14. B 15. D

Unit 6

Ex. 1, p. 43: 1. for/by 2. with 3. to 4. of 5. on 6. of 7. to/with 8. for 9. for 10. to 11. at/by 12. to/with 13. about/with (Article 3 is the true story)

Ex. 2, p. 43: Answers will vary.

Ex. 3, p. 44: excited on → excited about, happened about → happened to, talk for → talk to/with, complain with → complain about, accustomed for → accustomed to, ask to someone → ask someone, thank you to → thank you for

Ex. 4, p. 45: Answers will vary but should have these phrases in them: 1. count on 2. give to 3. approve of 4. (be) full of 5. (be) done with 6. (be) proud of 7. consist of

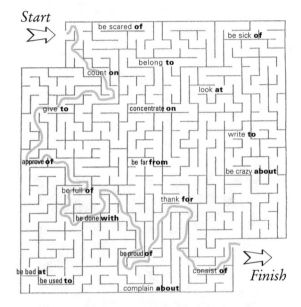

Ex. 5, p. 46: 1. talk to/with 2. am aware of 3. happened to 4. is famous for 5. depend on 6. look for 7. think of

Ex. 6, p. 46: 1. acd 2. abd 3. ac 4. c 5. acd 6. abcd 7. ac 8. ac

Ex. 7, p. 48: 1. c 2. c 3. d 4. d 5. b 6. c 7. a 8. b 9. C 10. D 11. A 12. B 13. A 14. B 15. A

Unit 7

Ex. 1, p. 51: 1. You must keep your seatbelt fastened at all times. 2. You store your carry-on baggage under the seat or in the overhead compartment. 3. The flight attendants will show the film *You've Got Mail* after the meal. 4. You will find your luggage in the baggage claim area. 5. You can call a flight attendant by pushing the button over your head. 6. The flight attendants will serve your meal once we reach cruising altitude.

Ex. 2, p. 52: (Each answer has two sentences. The second sentence of each answer will vary.) 1. The Eiffel Tower was built by Alexandre-Gustave Eiffel. 2. The part of James Bond was/is played by Pierce Brosnan. 3. How many plays were written by William Shakespeare? 4. This computer was designed for children. 5. The assembly line was first used in Henry Ford's factory. 6. Katy was embarrassed when she fell down the stairs.

7. We were surprised by the end of the movie.
8. When was the famous cathedral completed?

Ex. 3, p. 53: Last night I saw a movie that everyone in the nation must see! Nikki Coleman and Red Manly beautifully play the lead roles of Julianna and Rolf. A neighbor kidnaps Julianna, and someone assigns Rolf to her case. Grief overcomes Julianna's mother, and she is unable to assist Rolf in his pursuit of her beloved daughter. Surprising twists and turns make the movie believable. If you want to know the ending, ask someone to take you to this movie. It is a must see! Four stars!

Ex. 4, p. 54:

Ex. 5, p. 55: Answers will vary.

Ex. 6, p. 56: 1. d 2. bcd 3. abc 4. acd 5. abd 6. bc 7. acd 8. bc

Ex. 7, p. 57: 1. d 2. c 3. d 4. a 5. d 6. a 7. d 8. a 9. A 10. C 11. A 12. D 13. A 14. A 15. C

Unit 8

Ex. 1, p. 60: Answers will vary. Suggested answers: 1. This is a person who is older than sixty. 2. This is a person who enjoys life. 3. This is a person whose child makes good grades. OR This is a person who has a smart child. 4. This is a person who has grandchildren. OR This is a person who is proud of his/her grandchildren. 5. This is a person who likes rock and roll music. 6. This is a person who is crazy about sailing.

Ex. 2, p. 61: 1. The man wrote a famous novel that is about life on an island in the Pacific. 2. The farmer who (that) had a very bad harvest had to sell his land. 3. Lindsey just bought a new textbook that (which) teaches molecular biology. 4. The girl whose cousin is visiting her from New Zealand is beginning to pick up a New Zealand accent. 5. Jonathan likes to listen to music that (which) has a good beat and is easy to dance to. 6. The boy whose new car is fast and expensive had a bad automobile accident. 7. April likes to cook food that (which) is spicy and exotic.

8. Michael wrote an angry letter to the woman who (that) is president of a computer company.

Ex. 3, p. 62: Possible answers: 1. The tenant who has waited the longest is Robert Johnson. 2. Tony Maruzzi's apartment is the one that has a stopped up sink. 3. The sliding glass door is the one that needs to be fixed. 4. The apartment with the most urgent problem is Tony Maruzzi's. OR Tony Maruzzi's apartment is the one with the most urgent problem. 5. She is the tenant whose apartment has air conditioning problems. OR She is the tenant in whose apartment the air conditioning doesn't work.

Ex. 4, p. 63:

Ex. 5, p. 64: 1. who (that) robbed the bank 2. who (that) was wearing a red jacket 3. whom (that) he was speaking to 4. which (that) was very tight 5. which (that) was stuffed full of money

Ex. 6, p. 64: 1. abc 2. ac 3. abcd 4. c 5. ad 6. abc 7. bc 8. abd

Ex. 7, p. 66: 1. a 2. d 3. c 4. d 5. a 6. b 7. b 8. d 9. C 10. B 11. B 12. C 13. D 14. B 15. D

Unit 9

Ex. 1, p. 69: to begin, to make, talking, working, typing, to sell, calling, hearing

Ex. 2, p. 69: 1. We expect to graduate by next year. 2. The students finished taking the test two hours ago. 3. Do you want to go swimming tomorrow afternoon? 4. Children often enjoy going to the circus. 5. My parents would like to visit Peru. 6. You shouldn't put off studying for next week's test. 7. Carlos and Laura postponed getting married until next year. 8. Tina offered to give me a ride after class last night.

Ex. 3, p. 70: to do, to make, watching, to eat, to contact, to be, using, to give

Ex. 4, p. 71: 1. to play, Pelé, 2. getting, Switzerland 3. getting, Madonna 4. to become, Corazón Aquino 5. to resign, Richard Nixon 6. to become OR becoming, Leonardo DiCaprio 7. dancing, Brazil 8. to host, South Korea and Japan

Ex. 5, p. 72: Answers will vary.

Ex. 6, p. 72: 1. bc 2. b 3. bc 4. a 5. d 6. cd 7. c 8. b
Ex. 7, p. 74: 1. d 2. b 3. d 4. b 5. c 6. a 7. d 8. d
  9. A 10. C 11. A 12. C 13. D 14. A 15. B

Unit 10

Ex. 1, p. 77: Answers may vary: I want to <u>attend</u> <s>the</s>
Lantic University so that I can earn a degree in
civil engineering. I have <u>been</u> studying advanced
math for several years<u>;</u> therefore, I think that I
<u>will</u> do very well in your program. One of my
weaknesses is reading<u>,</u> but I have strong time
management skills, and I <u>always</u> allow plenty of
time to complete <u>reading</u> assignments. My father
is an engineer, and I want to become one, <u>too,</u> so
that I can work at his company when I <u>graduate</u>.

Ex. 2, p. 77: 1. I went to Rome in order to (answers
will vary here) 2. I want to study English because
(answers will vary here) 3. Rosa wants to see Eric
Clapton, and Jose does too. 4. Gary was in Idaho
last year, and Henry was too. 5. Sandra doesn't
know how to speak English, and Linda doesn't
either. 6. Mary swims every day, but Joe doesn't.
7. Nancy drives to school; however, Oscar walks.
8. I brought three pencils so I would have enough.

Ex. 3, p. 78: Answers will vary.

Ex. 4, p. 79:

Ex. 5, p. 80: Answers will vary.

Ex. 6, p. 81: 1. cd 2. b 3. ad 4. cd 5. d 6. abd 7. d
  8. cd

Ex. 7, p. 82: 1. c 2. a 3. c 4. a 5. c 6. b 7. a 8. a
  9. D 10. C 11. A 12. D 13. D 14. B 15. D

Unit 11

Ex. 1, p. 85: introduce a new sound to you, explain
the pronunciation to you, open your mouths for
me, pronounce the words for you, repeat the
words to me, answer a question for you

Ex. 2, p. 85: 1. I gave the book to Lisa. 2. The teacher
didn't explain the lesson to me. 3. The bank teller
cashed a check for my mother. 4. My manager introduced me to his wife. 5. Can you describe your
country to me? 6. The police officer asked us some

questions. 7. The plane ticket cost him 500 dollars.
8. Thelma offered me a ride home after class.

Ex. 3, p. 86: 1. me 2. them 3. to me 4. them
  5. them 6. them 7. to Dad and Mom 8. me

Ex. 4, p. 87: Answers will vary. Suggested answers:
  1. Italy, Turkey 2. Florida 3. 1998 4. Giza
  5. Twentieth century 6. England 7. Possible
  answers: Arabic, Japanese, Hebrew 8. California,
  Florida, Texas

Ex. 5, p. 87: Answers will vary.

Ex. 6, p. 88: 1. ab 2. bcd 3. abcd 4. b 5. bd 6. c
  7. ab 8. ad

Ex. 7, p. 89: 1. a 2. b 3. a 4. d 5. c 6. b 7. c 8. a
  9. B 10. B 11. D 12. D 13. C 14. C 15. D

Unit 12

Ex. 1, p. 92: T; Chocolate has not been proven to
cause cavities or tooth decay. 2. F; When Christopher Columbus was visiting what is now Honduras, he found a Spanish ship with cocoa beans
in it. 3. T; The fruit of the cocoa tree is white on
the inside and green on the outside. 4. T; Chocolate consists of saturated fat, which can cause
heart disease. 5. T; Chocolate companies were
worried about recent research because they
thought they would have to put a health warning
label on their products.

Ex. 2, p. 93: 1. Did you take out the garbage? 2. I
was watching TV when the pizza came. 3. Julia
has never traveled to Japan. 4. You must drive
carefully so you don't get into an accident. 5. The
tree was decorated by the children. 6. That is the
boy that I met last year. 7. I like to read books in
order to learn about different countries. 8. My
parents bought me a new car.

Ex. 3, p. 94: Answers will vary.

Ex. 4, p. 95:

Ex. 5, p. 97: Answers will vary.

Ex. 6, p. 98: 1. bcd 2. a 3. b 4. abd 5. ac 6. a 7. ac
  8. bcd

Ex. 7, p. 99: 1. c 2. d 3. d 4. b 5. d 6. c 7. d 8. b
  9. D 10. A 11. A 12. C 13. C 14. B 15. A